Mordecai Cubitt Cooke

British Edible Fungi

How to Distinguish and how to Cook them

Mordecai Cubitt Cooke

British Edible Fungi
How to Distinguish and how to Cook them

ISBN/EAN: 9783744775953

Printed in Europe, USA, Canada, Australia, Japan

Cover: Foto ©Lupo / pixelio.de

More available books at **www.hansebooks.com**

BRITISH EDIBLE FUNGI

HOW TO DISTINGUISH AND HOW TO COOK THEM

WITH COLOURED FIGURES OF UPWARDS OF FORTY SPECIES

BY

M. C. COOKE, M.A., LL.D., A.L.S.

AUTHOR OF " HANDBOOK OF BRITISH FUNGI ;" " ILLUSTRATIONS OF
BRITISH FUNGI ;" "FUNGI, THEIR NATURE, USES," ETC.

LONDON

KEGAN PAUL, TRENCH, TRÜBNER & CO. Ltd.

PATERNOSTER HOUSE, CHARING CROSS ROAD

1891

PREFACE.

FUNGUS eating is on the increase, thanks to Field clubs and their fungus forays, but the complaint has been heard for many years that no efficient handbook for the guidance of young or inexperienced mycophagists could be found in the English language. One or two laudable attempts have been made, but they have left much to be desired, and for the past ten years my fungus eating friends have continued to urge me, as one of the oldest of fungus eaters, to give the results of my experience. Admirable as Dr Badham's book was when published, and fully as it answered its purpose then, no one will contend that it is " up to date." However, the world is large enough for both of us. The list given at the end will represent all the kinds that I remember to have eaten, and as sixty-five will be considered sufficient to establish my claim to be a fungus eater, it may also be regarded as sufficient to exonerate me from any charge of presumption or inexperience. It has usually been the custom to include poisonous and edible fungi in one book, but from this custom I have diverged, for two or three reasons. It is not commendable to popularize knowledge of vegetable poisons easy to procure. It is not advisable to mix the descriptions and figures of good and bad species without distinct labelling, as on a chemist's bottle, of "poison" across each noxious species. And it is *not* desirable to increase the bulk and cost of a little book which was intended in furtherance of "fungus eating." Copious notes have been added on the preparation of the different species for the table, some old and some new, but all practical. By the aid of the descriptions in writing, as untechnical as possible, and the coloured figures, it is hoped that all reasonable care has been taken to prevent error, or danger, in eating mushrooms or toadstools. If I have rendered the art of fungus eating easier or safer I shall have accomplished my object.

M. C. COOKE.

LONDON, 1891.

CONTENTS.

8 CONTENTS.

EXPLANATION OF PLATES.

EXPLANATION OF PLATES.

BRITISH EDIBLE FUNGI.

I.—FUNGUS EATING.

FUNGUS eating is not a modern idiosyncrasy confined to a few enthusiasts, or limited to a few Western States of Europe. It is ancient in its origin, and of wide geographical distribution. If we seek for traces of the practice amongst ancient nations we shall be convinced of its antiquity. In some of the Talmudical treatises mention is made of fungi which were allowed as food. In one treatise it is asked, "With what blessing are fungi to be consecrated before being eaten?" and, again, we are informed that if a person was under a vow not to eat of the fruits of the earth, this did not prevent him from eating fungi, as such things did not derive nourishment from the soil but from the viscid matter of trees. In another of the treatises it is said that "The people went out into the fields, and gathered for themselves fungi and boleti." And there are also Chaldee words which are equivalent to *fungi* and *boleti*. This carries the eating of fungi backwards

to some of the most ancient of civilized peoples.
Amongst the old Greeks fungi were certainly eaten,
for Athenæus quotes various authors on the subject.
He says there are not many kinds which are good
to eat, and that the greater part of them produce
a choky sensation.   Another author says, " You
will be choked, like those who waste away by eating mushrooms," showing that even then there were
persons prejudiced against them.   The Romans, too,
indulged in the same habits, for there are various
allusions in Latin authors to different kinds of fungi.
Boleti were in special favour, and truffles next in
esteem.   One writer declares that the former were so
exquisite that it was not safe to send them anywhere
by messenger, for he would be sure to eat them by
the way.   You might send silver and gold, but not
boleti.

> Argentum atque aurum facile est, laenamque togamque,
> Mittere : boletos mittere difficile est.

We read that special vessels (*boletaria*) were used in
which to cook the "boleti."   Martial represents one
of these as complaining of a degraded use to which it
had been applied.   It was designed for cooking
mushrooms.   Alas! it now cooked cabbage sprouts.
How often has it been stated, and repeated, that a
dish of boleti concealed the poison which Locusta
administered to Claudius ?   These boleti were not the
same as now called by that name, but agarics, of

which Dr Badham declares that the "royal boletus" served to Cæsar was the *Agaricus Cæsarea*, so called in honour of the event.

Allusions to fungi in the ancient classics have been so admirably collated and detailed by the Rev. W. Houghton,[1] that it is only necessary to allude to his treatise as the most complete and exhaustive on this subject in any European language. Nevertheless there are one or two quotations specially applicable to fungus eating to which reference may be made here. Celsus says, "If any one shall have eaten noxious fungi let him eat radishes with vinegar and water, or with salt and vinegar; these may be distinguished from the wholesome kinds by their appearance, and can be rendered serviceable by a mode of cooking them." Dioscorides alludes also to edible fungi, for he writes : " Some people say that the bark of the white and the black poplar, when cut into small pieces and scattered over dunged spaces, will produce edible fungi at all seasons."

Pliny has a great deal to say about fungi, and amongst his other observations he writes: " I will now make some general observations on the cooking of fungi, because this is the only food which dainty voluptuaries themselves prepare with their own hands, and thus, as it were, by anticipation feed on them, using amber knives and silver service. Those

[1] "Notices of Fungi in Greek and Latin Authors," by Rev. W. Houghton, M.A., in *Ann. Nat. Hist.*, Jan. 1885.

kinds which remain hard after cooking are injurious, while those which admit of being thoroughly well cooked, when eaten with saltpetre are harmless ; they are rendered more safe still if they are cooked with meat, or with pear stalks; indeed, it is good to eat pears immediately after fungi. Vinegar being contrary to them neutralizes their dangerous qualities. All these products appear after showers." Our purpose being served, by these quotations, to show that edible fungi were known to the ancients, we leave the rest of Mr Houghton's excellent chapter untouched.

Without waiting to demonstrate that in more recent times they are consumed throughout Europe to a far greater extent than in the British Isles, from Russia and Kamtchatka to Austria and Italy, in Germany, Belgium, France, Switzerland, and in Sweden, Norway, and Denmark, we follow the practice to the United States of North America, where kinds are eaten, according to Dr Curtis, to which we take exception. He enumerates altogether one hundred and thirty excellent species. During the latter part of the great civil war, the people of the Southern States, being much pressed for food, found fungi of very great importance to them. In the Rocky Mountains other species come in for consumption. Finishing first with the Northern Hemisphere, we find fungus eating on the slopes of the Himalayas ; dried morels sold for food in the bazaars of North

Western India; special kinds of agaric, not unlike
our own St George's mushroom, universally considered as a delicacy in Afghanistan; other species
known and appreciated in the Punjab, and some others
even in Southern India. It is stated in the *Edinburgh Review* (April 1869), "We have been informed
by a gentleman who has lived many years in India
that the natives seem to eat fungi promiscuously,
chopping up the different species together, without
any ill effects." In the Malay Peninsula, Penang,
and the Straits settlements dried fungi are an article
of commerce. Seven distinct species are recognised
by natives, and eaten at Penang, whilst in China and
Japan, especially in China, there is a considerable
import trade of dried fungi for soup, as well as an
artificial cultivation of similar species in the interior.
A large kind of hedgehog mushroom (*Hydnum*) is
eaten fresh or dried in Japan, and is an article of
internal trade. One of the dried species from South
Eastern Asia grows on trees, and is not unlike *Agaricus ulmarius*. In many parts of Asia the common
mushroom is also found, according to the testimony
of Europeans, and is eaten by the natives.

Southwards, in the New World, fungi are eaten in
various countries. In Tierra del Fuego they are for
several months the staple food of the country. One
of the tree morels (*Cyttaria*) is called "summer
fruit," and is very common on beech trees. It is
eaten systematically. A native, when asked what

they had to eat, replied, " Plenty of fish and too much summer fruit." Another species is found and eaten at Cape Horn. In Brazil some species of agaric, closely allied to the common mushroom, are eaten ; and it seems that fungus eating is not unknown in Chili and Peru.

In Northern Africa some European and some indigenous species are employed as food. Of fungus eating on the western coast we know little, but at the Cape of Good Hope "The Parasol" and the "Common Mushroom" are found and eaten. Some of the native tribes are also mycophagists. At Natal a delicious agaric, called " Umkowaan," is highly appreciated. Throughout the whole of South Africa fungus eating is in favour, not only of well-known European species, but of some only known as native.

From New Zealand and Tahiti immense quantities of dried Jews' ears are exported to China, but there is no evidence that they are consumed in their native countries. Nevertheless there are other edible fungi in New Zealand which are articles of common consumption. The European "mushroom" is found and appreciated throughout the Australian colonies, as well as several indigenous species.

Having demonstrated that fungus eating is not a modern invention, or restricted to a few European localities, it may be asked, what reasons can be urged in its favour, and, in reply, we would suggest that it increases the variety of food resources, furnishes delicate condiments for less highly flavoured dishes, and might afford a nitrogenous meat-substitute in families of very restricted resources. The chief requisite for ensuring these results is the wider diffusion of useful information. In illustration we will quote some pertinent remarks by Dr Curtis, applied by him to the United States, but capable of a wider application. "Hill and plain, mountain and valley, woods, fields, and pastures swarm with a profusion of good, nutritious fungi, which are allowed to decay where they spring up, because people do not know how, or are afraid, to use them. By those of us who know their use, their value was appreciated, as never before, during the late war, when other food, especially meat, was scarce and dear. Then such persons as I have heard express a preference for mushrooms over meat had generally no need to lack grateful food, as it was easily had for the gathering, and within easy distance of their homes, if living in the country. Such was not always the case, however. I remember once, during the gloomy period when there had been a protracted drought, and fleshy fungi were to be found only in damp, shaded woods, and but few even there, I was unable to find enough of any one species for a meal, so, gathering of every kind, I brought home thirteen different kinds, had them all cooked together in one grand *pot pourri*, and made an excellent supper."

This is further corroborated by an incident narrated by the Rev. M. J. Berkeley. "Our schoolmaster," he says, "was a person of some scientific information. At a time when he could not afford to buy meat, he told me himself that he kept his family for several months upon different species of mushrooms. He was a person who was able to distinguish between that which was good and that which was bad, and he collected them himself."

If we have not made out a case for fungus eating, it is not from any lack of feeling in favour of it. From experience we have learnt that preaching is not half so successful as practice in carrying conviction, and we doubt if we have not made more converts by prevailing upon them to eat of dishes set before them at our instigation, than by writing up their virtues in books. There is always a latent timidity, at least in most minds, of committing a mistake, and being poisoned; or else there is a scepticism that substitutes are never so good as originals. In this case the error consists in regarding as *substitutes* for mushrooms viands which are not proposed as substitutes, but as supplementary. Fungus eaters do not appreciate the ordinary mushroom the less because they can eat of fifty other kinds "without fear and trembling," and without any question of competition being present in their minds. As in nature there is endless variety in form and colour, so in fungi there is great variety in flavour, instead of a uniform sameness. Let those who doubt read on, and profit by the succeeding chapters.

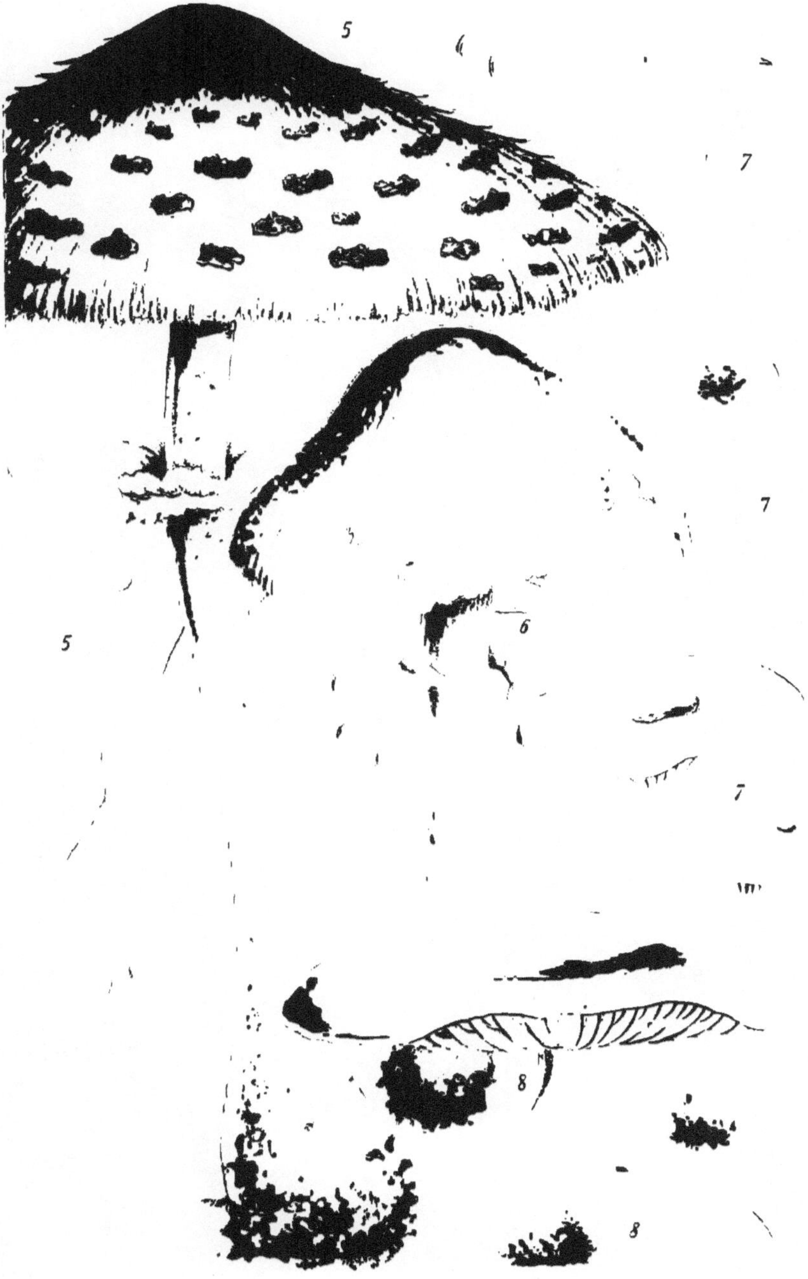
5
7
7
5
6
7
8
8

II.—EXPLANATORY.

NOTWITHSTANDING all the efforts which have been made during the past twenty years to diffuse information concerning the use of fungi as food, there still remains a vast amount of prejudice to overcome, and the necessity for the diffusion of knowledge is almost as great as ever. In the time of our grandfathers it was almost universally believed that our islands produced but one kind of fungus which was edible, and that was denominated the "mushroom;" all the rest were classed together as dangerous, and were only known as "toadstools." That this was a popular error has now come to be acknowledged, but hardly to the extent of admitting that we have not less than eighty different species which may be cooked and sent to table. A courageous lady of our acquaintance confesses to having cooked and eaten as many as sixty without the slightest accident or inconvenience. As may be expected, these are not all equally good, possessing a variety of flavour, and a difference of texture; and as tastes differ, so there will be a diversity of opinion as to relative merits, but, it being admitted that all are edible, it must be left to individual tastes to select those which please them best. Neither must it be expected that all are equally available for the same purposes, or are capable of

being prepared in the same manner. There is as
much art in cooking a fungus as in selecting one for
that purpose, although it is an art which, in both
cases, may be readily acquired.

If popular prejudice has, on the one hand, limited
the number of edible species to its lowest quantity, it
has, on the other hand, proportionately increased the
number of dangerous species to an alarming extent.
It was undoubtedly the prevailing opinion, not many
years ago, that every fungus was poisonous which was
not a veritable "mushroom." The lowest estimate
we can give of the number of species of gill-bearing
fungi, of the mushroom type, which have been found
in the British Islands, is eleven hundred, and yet of
these there are comparatively few which are known
to be positively dangerous. It is true that those
which are known are, for the most part, very virulent,
yet the number cannot be demonstrated to reach one
hundred. There are others, of course, which are
tasteless, insipid, bitter, or unpleasant, and unfit for
food, although not absolutely poisonous; but the
most alarming estimates have no foundation in fact.
It must always be remembered that a fungus which
may be perfectly harmless if cooked and eaten whilst
fresh would just as probably be deleterious if gathered
and kept for a day or two, without cooking. Chemical changes take place so rapidly that they cannot
be cooked too soon, and not even the common mushroom should be kept longer than possible. It would

be a good cardinal maxim always to "cook without
delay." Like the caution on the physic bottle,
"before taken to be well shaken," it is homely but
wholesome.

The question is often propounded, Is there no
general rule by which good or harmless fungi can be
distinguished from those which are deleterious? Many
attempts have been made to answer this question,
but none of them are satisfactory, except the negative
one, to the effect that no rule can be laid down which
shall be of universal application in the discrimination
of dangerous fungi. The only safeguard is to become
acquainted, by means of well-defined features, with
some of the best of the esculent species, and by no
means to experiment with those which are unknown.
It is true that this process will entail the trouble of
learning something, but better far to acquire the
necessary elementary information than run the risk
of mishap. We have always protested against foolish
risks, and cautioned would-be fungus eaters against
cooking and eating any kinds which they do not
know unmistakably. There is no difficulty in
recognising all the best kinds by means of ordinary
intelligence and care, and, when once known, so as to
be distinguished from others somewhat like them, or
from all the rest, then there is no fear of error. Good
fungi have usually a pleasant mushroomy odour, a
smell of new meal, a faint scent resembling anise, or
no particular odour at all. Then, again, a fragment

broken off from the freshly-gathered fungus, if tasted, should possess an agreeable nutty flavour, with no acridity, sharpness, or tingling upon the tongue. And, further, it is a most suspicious indication of bad qualities if a fungus when broken, cut, or bruised speedily turns of a deep blue or greenish colour. Avoid, therefore, all fungi with a disagreeable odour, a pungency of flavour, and a tendency to become blue when bruised.

In order to facilitate our progress hereafter, and to prevent repetition, it will be advisable at once to explain the general features of a gill-bearing fungus, of the mushroom type, with as little technicality as possible. When these few simple terms are thoroughly comprehended they can be alluded to without explanation. Annexed is the outline of a section cut through a fungus of the above kind, from top to bottom. It will often be found very useful and instructive to cut down such fungi as may be met with, and compare the one with the other, carefully noting the minute differences. In the woodcut *a* is the *pileus*, or cap, and *b* the *stem* which supports it. The under side of the pileus, or cap, is occupied by a series of parallel plates, or *gills*, *c*, which radiate from the stem to the margin of the cap. A little way down the stem is an indication, *d*, of the annulus, or *ring*, which adheres to and surrounds the stem. Some species have no ring, so that it is always of importance to ascertain at once if the individual

under examination has a ring or not. The stem is
sometimes solid throughout, and sometimes hollow
in the centre ; and in a few cases is so short as to be
scarcely visible.   There is sometimes a loose, or
fixed, *volva*, or sheath, at the base of the stem, but it
is only present in one or two species which are
edible, and is not shown in the woodcut.   In passing,

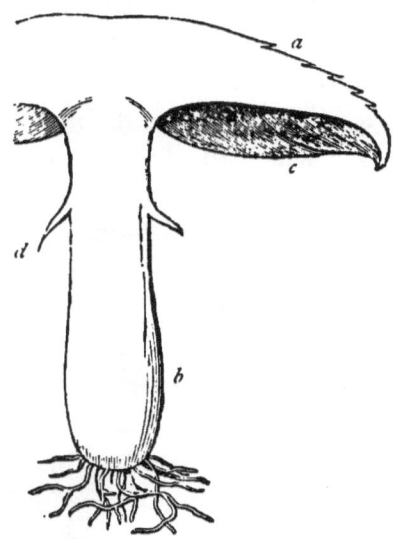

it may be remarked that, although the greater
number of fleshy fungi have the radiating plates, or
gills, on the under side of the pileus, or cap, yet there
are some in which the gills are replaced by tubes or
pores, or else by acute spines or teeth.

The gill-plates are variable in colour in different
species, and it is important that this colour should

always be observed. Having found your mushroom or toadstool, cut off the stem as close as possible to the gills, then place the pileus, with the gills down-wards, on a piece of paper, and let them remain for a few hours, or throughout the night. When re-moved, a very fine dust will be observed to have been thrown down on the paper from the gills. This dust consists of the spores (or seeds) of the fungus, which were produced on the naked gills, and have fallen when mature. This deposit of spores will either be white, salmon-coloured, brown, or tawny, dark brown, or black. In the common mushroom, for instance, they are of a dark purple brown. A great number of species which have purple brown spores are edible, whilst it is very rare indeed for a species with salmon-coloured spores to be worth eat-ing, and some are poisonous. The colour of the gills, and of the spores, are of considerable importance, and must be taken into account in determining a fungus.

When collecting fungi it is advisable to take into account where they were found growing, whether in woods, or in open lawns and pastures, because those which are found in woods are not found in the "open," and *vice versâ*. Again, those which habitually grow on rotting stumps and decayed trees, are to be rarely found elsewhere. Very few good edible species are to be found growing on trees.

There is an erroneous opinion extant, especially in rural districts, that all fungi which are good to eat grow on the ground in open places, and that if the cuticle or skin of the pileus cannot be peeled off easily it is unfit for food. Many excellent species will be found growing in woods, and the peeling of the cuticle is no general test.

Instances have been observed and recorded in which the same fungus, cooked and served at the same table, has been eaten and enjoyed without inconvenience by the majority of persons present, whereas one individual has been affected injuriously, and exhibited symptoms of fungus poisoning. We are personally acquainted with one man who can never eat a fragment of the ordinary mushroom, either by itself, or as a condiment, without suffering very severely in consequence. Such cases may be exceptional, but the good or bad qualities of the mushroom must not be determined by exceptional cases. Even cultivated mushrooms have been known to possess evil qualities when grown under peculiar conditions, or when they have become infested with a minute parasite. All fungi to be eaten should be well grown, clean, and fresh, and also cooked in such a manner as to be digestible, and not spoilt in the kitchen. These preliminary observations will enable us now to proceed with the details of species to be recommended, on the faith of a long personal experience.

III.—THE COMMON MUSHROOM.

IN most countries, and in past times as well as the present, the common mushroom (*Agaricus campestris*) has been held to occupy the place of honour amongst edible fungi. In Europe, Asia, America, and Australia it is equally esteemed, as it is, fortunately, thus widely distributed over the world, and readily recognized by natives or migrants, without fear or accident. That there are others equally good, and to some tastes better, is not yet an article of general faith, and so the " mushroom " continues to hold its reputation of pre-eminence. The roughest rustic, and the plainest of cooks, equally deem themselves capable of deciding between a "mushroom" and a "toadstool," and, truth to tell, seldom make any mistake. Whether it be necessary or not, it is expedient that we give a brief outline of its principal features for the discrimination of this fungus as found growing wild. The cultivated varieties differ a little in appearance, but are usually safe.

The mushroom is found growing amongst short grass in parks, lawns, and open places, and seldom exceeds three or four inches in diameter of the pileus, or cap, and often less. The stem is scarcely so long as the diameter of the pileus, and is proportionately thick. The upper part of the stem is encircled by

a collar or ring, like a frill, the outer edge of which is
at first united to the edge of the pileus, covering the
gills, and only breaks away as the pileus expands,
and then falls down to form the collar round the stem.
This ring is rather thin, and easily torn, so that sometimes it is brushed away, or falls, leaving behind only
a thin line, or scar, to show where it has been.　The
whole pileus and stem is of a creamy whiteness at first,
but becomes a little darker with age.　To the finger
the texture of the surface resembles that of a soft kid
glove, and the outer skin may be peeled off from the
margin upwards, nearly to the top, in flakes.　If this
fungus is cut through the middle of the pileus and
downwards through the stem, the flesh of the cap will
be seen to be thick, and white, sometimes turning a
little browner when cut.　To the taste it somewhat
resembles a filbert, tinged with a characteristic mushroom flavour.　The gill-plates, radiating from the stem,
do not grow to it, but are free from the stem, and of a
delicate pink colour, which they retain for some time,
changing at length, with age, to dark purple brown.
This is an excellent character to be observed and borne
in mind, that the pink gills of the young mushrooms
become dark purple brown.　There are ".toadstools"
(for so we may call them) which have the gills pink,
not changing to dark brown, and some of these are
dangerous. All good mushrooms (of this species)
should have the gills at first *pink*, nearly white when
in the "button" state, and at length dark purple

brown, and the spores which cover the gills are of the same colour. When the stem is cut off, and the cap laid gills downwards on a sheet of white paper for a few hours, or all night, the spores will fall on the paper in lines, and will appear almost black.

It is a popular error that mushrooms grow to their full size during a single night, and that they dissolve and vanish after the sun shines upon them. They are rapid in growth, and rapid in decay; but the same mushroom may be watched growing and expanding for two or three days, and then gradually decaying away. Much depends on the dampness or dryness of the season. In some seasons they are exceedingly plentiful, whilst at other times they are comparatively rare. This also is believed to depend chiefly on climatic conditions. It is not unusual for cultivated mushrooms to become attacked by a parasitic mould which renders them unfit for food. This misfortune rarely happens to the wild form, until it is in process of decay.

Stables, outhouses, and cellars may be utilised for the cultivation of mushrooms, and by ordinary care success is almost certain. They may be grown also in boxes and placed almost anywhere, so long as the temperature and humidity is attended to. The French are fond of growing them in cellars and caves. The catacombs of Paris are noted for their production of mushrooms in immense quantities. From the Méry caves as many as 3000 pounds are sometimes sent to market daily. In this country cave culture seems to be almost, if not quite, unknown. Bricks of mushroom spawn may be purchased of almost any seedsman, and if manure can be obtained, domestic cultivation might be much more common than it is. We have heard of a crop being grown in a hatbox, and we have seen them flourishing under the shelves in a greenhouse. Of course, some persons are far more successful than others, as is the case with flowering plants. Experience teaches wisdom.

The following method of cultivation has been recommended, and is often quoted :—" Collect a sufficient quantity of fresh horse-droppings, as free from straw as possible, lay it in an open shed in a heap, or ridge ; here it will heat violently, and in consequence should be now and then turned for sweetening. After this has subsided to moderation it will be in a fit state for forming into a bed. In the process of making the bed, the dung should be put on in small quantities, and beat firmly and equally together, until it is the required size. In this state let it remain until the highest degree of heat to which it is capable of coming is ascertained, which may be readily done by inserting a heat-stick, and pressing it with the hand ; if not found violent, the spawn may be broken up into pieces of two or three inches square, and put into holes about three inches in depth, by six inches asunder, over its surface ; after this, throw a very small quantity of well broken droppings over the whole. In this state let it remain for two or three weeks, when a loamy soil may be put on about an inch or an inch and a half thick, and gently patted with the spade. If the temperature of the house is kept about 60° or 65°, mushrooms may be expected in six weeks. It is not well to water the beds much, particularly when bearing." But nearly every good cultivator has his own method, or modification, and is prepared to believe chiefly in himself.

If there are different methods of cultivation, so there are different methods also of cooking mushrooms, the two old popular methods of grilling, or stewing, notwithstanding. Open grilling, or frying, is by no means to be recommended for any fungi, especially those of delicate flavour. The best plan is to lay them, when prepared, in a plate, or shallow dish, and cover them with another, and then place them in an oven, so that they are cooked gradually, and all the aroma and delicate flavour retained, all necessary adjuncts, such as butter, salt, pepper, or gravy having been added. When fried or grilled, whilst exposed, much of the aroma and flavour disappears up the chimney. A modification of the above method may thus be formulated :—Having picked a number of freshly-gathered mushrooms, cut them in pieces, wash in cold water, and dry them in a cloth. Put them in a pan, with butter, parsley, salt, and pepper ; cover closely, and place them over a brisk fire. When ready, add cream and yolk of egg to bind them together.

Some persons prefer, after cutting, to soak them in oil for one or two hours, add a piece of garlic instead of parsley, and cook as before. When ready, chopped parsley and lemon juice may be added.

Stewed mushrooms may be prepared by selecting the younger specimens, which are not fully expanded; wash in cold water, and dry with a cloth; chop quite finely, put them in a stewpan with a little butter and pepper; let them stand over a brisk fire, and when the butter is melted, squeeze in lemon juice, and add jelly broth, according to quantity; stew until reduced to the consistency of pea soup, and serve with meat, fish, or poached eggs.

A correspondent has kindly placed at our disposal a curious old formula copied from an old commonplace book of the early part of the seventeenth century. It is very interesting on account of its antiquity, and as such is worthy of a place in the present work.

"TO DRESS A DISH OF FUNGEE."

" Take them fresh gathered and put them betweene two dishes, and sett them on a Chaifing Dish of Coles, and there lett them Stewe, but put nothing to them in the first Stewing for they will Yeald Liquor enough of them selves, and When all the Water is

stewed out of them, power that Liquor Cleane from
them and put a good quantitye of Sallitt Oyle unto
them and Stewe them therein.   Wringe in the joyce
of one or two Leamons, or else putt in some Vinniger
and put in a little Nuttmegg and two or three Blades
of Mace.

"If your Lord or Lady Loves not Oyle, Stewe them
with a Little Sweete Butter and a little White
Wine."

Approved methods of cooking mushrooms are
known to every experienced cook, and need not be
repeated ; most persons believe them good almost
any way.   In the same manner mushroom catsup—
or, as locally called, "mushroom ketchup "—may be
readily manufactured.   Unfortunately, very much of
that decoction which is sold under the name of "catsup" is of questionable origin, and often innocent of
mushrooms.   Those who desire to possess good
"catsup" should make it for themselves, as the
process is easy.   To know whether "catsup" is
genuine, or only imitation, it is only necessary to
submit a drop to the microscope, and search for the
spores of the mushroom, which remain intact, *if
present*, and in considerable number.   Probably the
result will not be satisfactory when compared side by
side with the home made article.

IV.—THE MEADOW MUSHROOM.

NEXT in importance to the common mushroom, and often confounded with it, is the meadow mushroom (*Agaricus arvensis*), sometimes called, by way of distinction, the horse mushroom, a name most common in rural districts. Country people generally discriminate between these two species, and hold that whilst it is larger, and more imposing, the horse mushroom is not so good to eat, but that it is stronger and better for making ketchup than the genuine mushroom. There are some persons who contend that, for all purposes, the fuller flavour of the meadow mushroom makes it preferable to the smaller species found in parks and lawns, or by the roadside. The distinctions between them, beside the places in which they grow, are that the cap of the horse mushroom, when expanded, is sometimes as large as a dessert plate, often six inches, and quite smooth, having the texture of a good kid glove. They are more gregarious in habit, sometimes forming large rings, or parts of rings, and the gills are *not* at first pink, but dirty white. When cut or bruised the flesh turns yellowish brown, more or less deep, and in age the gills are almost black. This is the kind most commonly exposed for sale at greengrocers' shops in London and its vicinity, and undoubtedly is the fungus with which the ordinary Cockney is most practically acquainted. It certainly has a stronger odour than the true mushroom, and a stronger flavour, especially when raw. We have often found it very agreeable to gather and eat fresh young specimens of the mushroom, whilst the gills are still pink. Not only agreeable, but useful, for when abroad on a day's excursion, one or two of these raw specimens are an excellent substitute for sandwiches, as they satisfy hunger, are nutritive and digestible, and very pleasant and grateful to the palate. Young specimens of the horse mushroom may be eaten in the same manner, but in this state they are not so agreeable. Either of them may be sliced and placed inside a sandwich, as a sort of condiment, with good results. Persoon says that the horse mushroom is superior to the common mushroom ·in smell, taste, and digestibility, for which reasons it is generally preferred in France.

Allusion has already been made to the large size of this species. An instance has been recorded of a specimen weighing five pounds and six ounces and measuring forty-three inches in circumference. Withering, the botanist, mentions another which weighed fourteen pounds. We have had no experience of specimens exceeding ten or twelve inches in diameter, although we have been told that they will attain as much as twenty or twenty-four inches, but of this we must beg to remain sceptical.

There is something so characteristic in this, as well

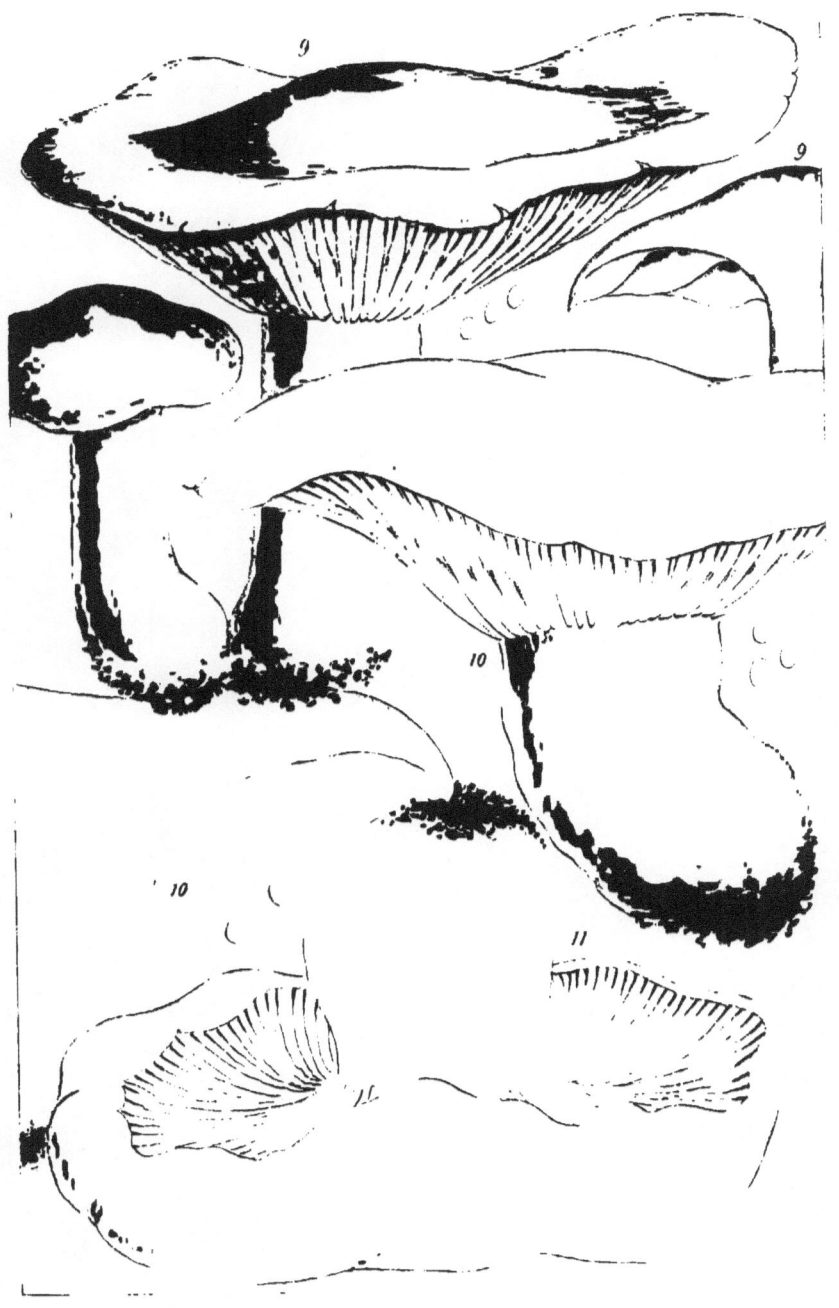

as the common mushroom, that we cannot help feeling surprise that anyone, with an ordinary amount of common-sense, should confound them with anything else. There is no other species found at the same season of the year and in the same localities with which it could be confused. In most cases of fungus poisoning which have come under notice there must have been recklessness or profound ignorance, for the fungi eaten, wherever identified, bear no resemblance to the common or the meadow mushroom. A cartoon was issued in one of the public journals a few years ago, in which a buxom damsel was represented as returning from collecting fungi, and meeting the Squire, who was in the act of cautioning her as to the result of her proceedings. "You can't be too particular—dangerous things, mushrooms." To which the damsel replies, " It doesn't much matter ; they're only for my mother-in-law." Cautions are proverbially useless now as well as in older times, when every little wood or coppice was adorned with a notice-board, on which was written, " Man-traps and spring-guns set here."

There is a large variety (called *villaticus*) of the meadow mushroom, which also attains ten or twelve inches in diameter, and is quite as good an article of food, but unfortunately it is rare. The principal difference resides in the surface of the cap or pileus, which is much darker, and broken up into a great number of flat scales; these are darker still, and lie

C

so flat as to appear to be glued down to the surface. This variety is mentioned here on account of the difference in its appearance, which would ensure its rejection by a careful person as not agreeing with our description of "a smooth, whitish cap, like a kid glove." The stem is often two inches thick, or even more, but short in proportion, and nearly solid. It is so rare a form that even those persons who are addicted to the study of fungi from year to year have most of them never seen it. It is needless to refer to similar rare varieties in a chapter of this kind, which is not intended for the professional fungus hunter, to whom alone they have any interest.

For some obscure reason this kind of mushroom has sometimes been called the St George's mushroom, and by this name it is believed to be known in Hungary, where the inhabitants regard it as the special gift of St George. But there is another, and quite a different mushroom, commonly found in this country in spring, to which the name "St George's mushroom" is applied with more reason, since it makes its appearance about the time of St George's Day. To this genuine St George we shall have to refer again in detail, and only allude to it here in order to protest against the horse mushroom being dedicated to the saint.

Several different kinds of fungi have had the credit of forming "fairy-rings" on the grass in meadows, and the horse mushroom is one of these, from its habit of often growing in rings, but it is not the real Fairy Ring champignon.

In all matters of cooking the same processes may be used indiscriminately for the common mushroom and the horse mushroom. In addition to the recommendations in the chapter devoted to the common mushroom, we may give a few others for the sake of variety. The novelty of potted mushrooms may be secured by selecting small open specimens, which should be trimmed of their stems, and rubbed; a quart of these with three ounces of butter, two teaspoonfuls of salt, half a teaspoonful of a mixture of cayenne pepper and ground mace, or grated nutmeg, should be stewed for ten or fifteen minutes, or until the mushrooms are tender. Take them out and drain them on a sloping dish, and when cold press them into small pots, and pour clarified butter over them, in which state they will keep for a week or two. If required to be kept longer writing paper must be cut to the size and laid over the butter, and melted suet poured over it. In this manner they may be kept several weeks in a cool dry place.

Pickled mushrooms are a favourite with some persons, although others may object to them on the ground that they lose so much of their flavour in the process as to be scarcely recognisable. It is usual to select those which are called "button mushrooms" in which the edge of the cap is not parted from the stem, but retains still its globose shape. The stems are cut off short, so that the fungus resembles a little white ball, perhaps not more than an inch in diameter. They should be rubbed quite clean, and laid in salt and water for forty-eight hours. Sufficient vinegar should be boiled with black pepper and mace, with a clove or two, and then stood aside till quite cold. The mushrooms should be packed closely in wide-mouthed bottles, a little pepper sprinkled over them, and then covered with the vinegar, and corked close. In this manner they should keep for years.

There is an old-fashioned method which is simple and excellent for the large horse mushroom. It consists in peeling off the cuticle of the cap, and then cutting the stem close to the gills. Lay them with the gills upwards in a shallow dish, sprinkle with salt and pepper, and place a lump of butter in the centre of each. Cover close and place in an oven. Or, in default of this, cook in an enamelled frying pan, keeping them still covered until done. When ready serve on toast.

Stuffed mushrooms are recommended by a French author to be thus prepared. Take mushrooms of a medium size, and prepare for them at the same time the following stuffing. A piece of butter, grated bacon, some bread crumbs, sweet herbs, garlic, according to taste, salt, coarse pepper, and the least morsel of spice; when these are all well mixed, turn over the mushrooms with the gills upwards, clear away the stems and fill the hollow with this stuffing; then wrap each in paper, and cook them in a pan, adding a spoonful of oil as occasion may require. If preferred, a few slices of fowl or game may be added.

Doubtless it would not be difficult to collect together one hundred recipes for cooking mushrooms, but this is not our present duty. We have furnished sufficient for ordinary use, and feminine ingenuity may suggest others. It cannot be too often repeated that the fresher the mushrooms are at the time of cooking the better will be the result. A connoisseur will detect, almost at once, the difference between the flavour of the common and the horse mushroom. And so with all other species; no two of them are precisely the same, so that, when other species are recommended, it must not be presumed that, when cooked, they will be precisely like the mushroom, because they will be precisely different.

V.—BROWN MUSHROOMS.

UNDER the title of "Brown Mushrooms" we must have a few words to say on two or three kinds, which resemble in many points the ordinary mushroom, are equally excellent, but are unfortunately by no means common.

SCALY BROWN MUSHROOM (*Agaricus Elvensis*).— We have never had the good fortune to meet with this kind of mushroom more than three or four times ; and then it was collected under the drip of large oak trees in pastures. It was first of all found in this country, but has since been met with in France. For size it exceeds the common mushroom, but is scarcely so large as the horse mushroom, and usually grows gregariously, a number together, though not forming a ring. It differs from both the above in being much darker coloured, almost purplish brown, with the top of the cap, or pileus, broken up into large brown scales, which are somewhat conical towards the margin. This scaly cap gives it a most remarkable appearance, but the odour is so " mushroomy " that it would at once be supposed to be a near relation of the mushroom, notwithstanding the great difference in appearance. The gills at first are of a brownish flesh colour, becoming dark purplish brown, like those of the mushroom, with age. The ring around the stem is large, warted on the under side, but soon hanging down like a turn-down collar. When cut through the cap the thick, firm flesh will be found of a dirty white, but not changing colour, or very slightly, on exposure to the air. When fully expanded the cup is generally five or six inches in diameter, and the stem is proportionately robust.

The flavour, when cooked, has been strongly commended by all who have experienced it. Some have gone so far as to declare it superior to the finest mushroom ever eaten, and all have confessed it in every way equal to the best. It has not, like many edible species, a flavour peculiar to itself, but entirely of the mushroom kind, resembling the cultivated varieties rather than the wild ones, and not so strongly flavoured as the horse mushroom. The mode of cooking is precisely that of ordinary mush- rooms, but we decidedly prefer them grilled or fried with butter, and served on toast. We have only found them in the latter part of August and begin- ning of September, and never singly but always in sufficient number to furnish half a dozen persons with a satisfactory breakfast. Although we never have failed to search the same spot, year by year, at the same period, we have been disappointed, in some seasons, in finding no trace of them; but in succeed- ing years they have appeared again.

BLEEDING BROWN MUSHROOM (*Agaricus hæmorr- hoidarius*).—Although this fungus is often found at the foot of oaks, yet we have never met with it in open pastures, but always in woods, chiefly by the side of roads, and paths, running through woods, and never more than two or three together, often solitary. In appearance it differs from the above, in that the colour is almost that of the ground on which it grows, so that it may be passed over as a lump of soil, when not fully expanded. The colour may be described as wholly of a dirty brown, something like brick earth, or clayey soil, and the pileus is not so distinctly scaly as the foregoing, the scales being smaller, and more closely pressed to the flesh. It cannot by any means be termed attractive, especially as it turns darker, and lurid, wherever pressed or bruised, and when cut or broken becomes of a dull blood-red. We have seldom seen it exceed four or five inches in diameter, and often less. The stem is generally a little swollen at the base, and of a dirty light brown colour, as well as the large pendulous ring. The gills are at first flesh-coloured, with a rosy tinge, but at length become of a dark purple umber, scarcely different from that of the common mushroom. We have no knowledge of any species with which this could possibly be confounded, if the change of colour to lurid red when cut or bruised is borne in mind. It is true that there are others with a tinge of red on the stem, but none in which it takes the appearance of bleeding when wounded. It may be taken for granted that this also is a rare species, or at any rate a sporadic and local one, and if it were not so remarkable, and such excellent eating, would scarcely warrant a notice.

Nothing can be added of methods of preparing this species for the table at all different from those in vogue for the common mushroom. We do not recognize anything peculiar in its flavour, which could distinguish it from the mushroom. It is not so juicy or delicate flavoured as the scaly brown mushroom, but, for all that, it is entirely of the mushroom type, and even a connoisseur would fail to distinguish them. There is a variety of the common mushroom described by Berkeley, under the name of *rufescens*, which is said to grow in pastures, the flesh of which turns a bright red when bruised. The gills of this variety are described as quite white when young. We have never seen anything like this, and suspect that it may have been some accidental variety, or at any rate such a rare occurrence that it has never appeared again.

WOOD MUSHROOM (*Agaricus silvaticus*).—This is by no means uncommon in woods, but scattered and solitary, or seldom more than two or three together. It is hardly like the ordinary mushroom in appearance, and hence is often a puzzle to young fungus hunters. The stem is thin and lanky, usually a little thickened at the base, and, when cut, it exhibits a hollow, like a tube, down the centre. The pileus is brown and fibrous, or covered with little darker scales, and the flesh is thinner than in any of the species we have as yet enumerated. The most common size is for the pileus to be about three inches across, and the stem five or six inches high, and scarcely half an inch thick, except at the base. The ring round the stem is thin, like a membrane, becoming dark brown, and situated at a considerable distance down the stem, so that it is at length but little above the middle, between the under side of the cap and the ground. The gills are thin and crowded, and have rather a reddish tinge at first, but very soon turn brown, and are ultimately as dark as in the horse mushroom. The stem is always whitish, or yellowish white, except when stained with the spores. Unluckily insects are fond of it, and the pileus and top of the stem, when mature, are generally "maggoty."

This is but little inferior to the mushroom in its edible qualities, although we can scarcely consider it equal to that, or either of the above named. It is deficient in aroma, and not so delicate in flavour, and as the pileus is thin, there is very little flesh when cooked ; but it may be accepted as a substitute for the mushroom, and may be mixed with other species in the preparation of "ketchup." There are no special methods of cooking it, except, it may be said scarcely to merit stewing, and to be unfit for pickling.

This concludes what we may term the *true* mushroom group of edible species, in which the flavour is all similar but differing chiefly in delicacy or intensity. There are therefore five species worthy of recommendation, namely, the common mushroom, growing in parks, pastures, or lawns ; the horse mushroom, found usually in meadows or damp pastures ; the scaly brown mushroom, growing in company under the drip of oak trees ; the bleeding mushroom found by roadsides in woods ; and the wood mushroom not uncommon under trees in woods. To all these we may add the cultivated varieties of the common mushroom, which are raised artificially from mushroom spawn. In all these the spores are small, elliptical, and of a very dark brown, almost black colour ; indeed they seem to be black when thrown down upon white paper, but decidedly brown when viewed by transmitted light under the microscope.

When alluding to some of the modes of cooking, as applied to the common mushroom, we omitted mention of one which will commend itself to all whose stomachs will bear rich food, without fear of bilious results. It consists in cleaning and slicing up the mushrooms, and boiling, or stewing them very gently in milk—just enough to cover them. When sufficiently stewed add salt and spice, a lump of butter, and thicken with good thick cream ; stir them well together and serve. Wherever the richness of the dish is no obstacle, this will be found an improvement on the old method of stewing in water, and thickening with flour, or even to stewing in gravy or stock. Let no one blame the mushrooms in the event of this dish disagreeing with them, since it must be evident that it would be a rash venture with a delicate stomach.

VI.—SHAGGY CAPS.

A DECEASED friend always characterised the fungus about which we are now to write as "the fungus of civilization," and the reason alleged for this cognomen was that it was always to be found near human dwellings. There is no doubt of the fact that the fungus known by the scientific name of *Coprinus comatus* commonly makes its appearance, in the metropolitan area, on waste places and clearings which are being operated upon by the house-builder, so that it is in such spots that we invariably go in search of it for domestic purposes.

There is no universal common name for this characteristic fungus, although it has by some been called the "Maned Agaric" and the "Shaggy Caps." Perhaps the latter is as good an appellation as we could find, as will be manifest from the description. It is rarely found growing singly, but usually in clusters, bursting through the ground like the dirty white tops of pigeon's eggs ; but the cap or pileus is from the first elongated and cylindrical, and not egg-shaped or oval. When fully grown it will measure fully six inches from the ground to its apex, and often nine or ten inches. The cap itself seldom exceeds four or five inches, in shape almost like an extinguisher, with a rounded top, or rather an inverted tumbler, the diameter being less than half the height. The stem is long, erect, and a little tapering towards the top, nearly smooth, and quite white, from half an inch thick. The cap is dirty white, with a tinge of ochre on the top, covered with shaggy threads, which hang together like dependent scales, fringing also the edge of the cap. When cut down the centre the gill plates will be seen to be very broad and lanceolate, tapering to each extremity, reaching to the stem, but not attached to it. At first they are white, but soon become darker, with a lilac tint, towards the edge, and finally pass from a dingy purple to black. It is not unusual for the gills, when changing, to have a rosy tinge. There is one peculiarity which distinguishes this (and all species of *Coprinus*) from the true Agarics, and that consists in the gills, after full maturity, melting away into a black inky fluid, and falling in drops to the ground. After being some time gathered, even if immature, instead of drying up, the whole mass, excepting the stem, deliquesces, passing into a dark slimy mass. In this condition it has by no means a prepossessing appearance. Whilst fresh and firm it is neat, if not attractive, although usually fragments of the soil attach themselves to the pileus, reminding one of a dirty street Arab, to which it has some analogy. The spores are large, many times larger than those of the common mushroom, and very black. At the first there is a loose membranous collar, or ring, around the stem, but this soon disappears. It seems impossible for any person, in full possession of their senses, to confound this with any other known species, or if so, with one closely related to it, and equally harmless. We have many a time and oft been cautioned by the natives whilst collecting these fungi that they were only "nasty toadstools," and some have gone so far as to declare them "rank p'ison," although, in point of fact, they are far more universally wholesome than the ordinary mushroom, and have never been known to cause the slightest inconvenience.

For cooking purposes these fungi should be gathered before the gills turn black, although when quite black they may be converted into good "catsup." The caps being so commonly sandy, or sprinkled with fragments of soil, should be washed and then wiped dry, which process will remove most of the scaly threads. The cuticle will not peel off as in the mushroom. In flavour, when cooked in any way, it much resembles the mushroom, to which it is quite equal, if not superior. In one particular it possesses an advantage, since it is clearly more digestible, and less likely to disagree with persons of delicate constitutions. The old caution should not need repetition—always to cook all fungi as soon as possible after they are gathered, for then they are in their greatest perfection. Amongst the rural population there is a strong prejudice against this species which, in common with another to be presently referred to, are, almost more than any others, designated " toadstools " by way of contempt.

There is another fungus, closely related to the above, and resembling it in many particulars, which is equally edible, and nearly equal to it in flavour. The " Inky Mushroom " (*Coprinus atramentarius*) received that name because, when it becomes old, the gills melt away into a thick, black, inky fluid, which may be used as ink. In this respect it resembles the " Shaggy Caps " above described, only that perhaps it deliquesces rather more readily. It grows in dense clusters, mostly about old stumps, or from buried decayed wood, or, not unfrequently, by waysides, in gardens, and on lawns, without any suspicion of dead wood ; but it never grows on dung or manure. The cap is grey or slaty-colour, smooth and shining, often compressed laterally, and grooved. The top is generally rather dawny, sprinkled at first with small scales, and the margin rather lobed or scalloped. The gills are much the same as in the previous species, which it equals in size. Perhaps more than any other this is the victim of spiteful molestation by small boys and uneducated peasantry, for every exposed cluster is sure to be kicked about and destroyed almost as soon as it appears above ground. The reason for this may be found in the popular belief that it is a poisonous toadstool, and certainly when in the stage of decay it is not in the least inviting. Even when young the livid grey colour is not attractive, and the patches of dirt adhering to the cap help to render it only the more forbidding.

The edible qualities of this mushroom are by no means to be despised, especially when young, before the gills have changed colour; and after the latter have turned quite black, but the dripping stage has not commenced, either by themselves or mixed with others they will yield an excellent "catsup." Like the preceding, they are preferable stewed, or added to soups.

It has already been mentioned that the black fluid, caused by the melting of the gills, may be used as ink, when mixed with gum water, so as to ensure permanency. A curious proposal was made some years ago to utilize this ink for printing bank notes, and other documents subject to forgery. The advantage being that at any period of time, by moistening the letters, the large spores would appear quite distinctly under the microscope, and the genuine ink at once determined. Ordinary ink, having no such origin, would present no such appearance. To verify this, it is only necessary to write a word or two, by dipping a pen in the fluid dripping from the gills of a decaying *Coprinus*, allowing it to dry, and remain dry for a few days, then damp it, and either remove the ink by means of a clean camel-hair pencil to a glass slide, or examine *in situ*, with the microscope, and a quarter inch objective. Should such a sugges-

tion as this ever prove to be practicable, the "inky fungi" would secure a market-value beyond that which would accrue from their use as food. Hitherto, no successful effort has been made in the direction of cultivation of these species, because there has been no demand for them ; should such a demand arise, some sort of cultivation is not impossible.

VII.—PARASOL MUSHROOMS.

ALMOST the greatest, if not the greatest, favourite with fungus eaters is the "Parasol mushroom" (*Agaricus procerus*). It is certainly graceful and elegant in appearance, dry and clean to the touch, easily recognized, and, more than all, delicious at the table. Surely all the attributes are combined, and yet how few, except regular fungus eaters, know the "Parasol." It has a soft, spreading, regular cap, from three to seven inches broad, with a large boss or nipple standing up in the centre, of a dark brown colour, and broad, reddish brown scales disposed somewhat regularly over the rest of the surface, on a whitish, silky, fibrous substratum. The margin fringed with the ends of the threads. The stem slender, erect and graceful, from eight to ten inches in length, and not more than half-an-inch in thickness, swollen at the bottom into a distinct bulb, but

with no sheath. The lower part of the stem variegated with small closely pressed scales, and the
upper part adorned with a large conspicuous collar or
frill. This collar is apt to become loosened from its
attachment to the stem, and movable. The top of
the stem deeply sunk into the cap; the white gills
numerous, stopping short before reaching the stem,
so as to leave a naked space or groove around it;
smell and taste pleasant; such is the general appearance of this favourite mushroom, which occurs on the
ground, or amongst dead leaves, under trees amongst
grass, in the open, or on hedge banks, in late summer
or early autumn. Each individual grows by itself,
and not in clusters, but several are often found in the
neighbourhood of each other.

There is a companion species, which much resembles it (*Agaricus rachodes*), indeed, so much so
that some persons consider them only varieties. It
has been remarked that in some localities only
rachodes is found, and in others only *procerus*. It is
only necessary to point out the differences, for in
other points they will be found to agree. When
young the cap is more globose; the scales on the
mature cap are more persistent; the stem is free
from the snake-like markings at the base, and the
bulb at the base has a more distinct margin. There
is also a tendency in the flesh to become reddish or
brownish when cut or bruised. At one time, and
not so many years ago, this species was held to be

suspicious, and some taught that it was unwholesome, but this was undoubtedly a mere guess from the change of colour when broken. Practically there is no difference in their edible qualities, and we have eaten both of them many times and oft. Similar stations and the same season of the year produce both.

Another but more slender species is common in some localities, and not found at all in others (*Agaricus gracilentus*). It grows amongst grass by the roadside, but is thinner in the flesh, and not so much commended. There is a slight resemblance to the Parasol, but it is smaller, and the scales on the cap are much smaller and less conspicuous, the stem is thinner and almost white, with but a slight swelling at the base. There is no conspicuous brown apex to the cap, which is less pointed, and less fibrous in the cuticle and margin. The entire stature is about six inches, but the erect stem is scarcely thicker than a pipe stem. It is to be found about the same period of the year as the above, but would hardly be sought after provided the larger species could be obtained.

If it were not comparatively rare the fawn-coloured Parasol would compete with the true Parasol, in culinary value. But this (*Agaricus excoriatus*) is the rarest of the four species, and least like a parasol in shape. The cap is not more than $2\frac{1}{2}$ inches broad and of a general fawn colour. The cuticle is smooth

and thin, breaking up into irregular patches which
adhere to the cap. Beneath this broken cuticle the
surface is white and silky. The stem is about two
inches long, scarcely thickened at the base and
dirty white; near the top is a broad collar, which
readily separates and becomes movable. The whole
substance is soft and spongy, with very little odour.
It will be observed that it differs in general appearance from the other three kinds in having large irregular patches of the cuticle on the cap instead of
scales, and in a shorter, and proportionately shorter
stem. At first sight it would hardly seem to be
related to them. This is quite a summer species,
making its appearance about May or June, but not
after the end of August. Sometimes it is not recognized for years.

There are several other species of less note which
agree with the above in having a ring, and the white
gills scarcely reaching the stem, but their determination had better be left to the professed mycologist
as they are not of sufficient importance to be considered as regular edible species, and they require
good figures for their accurate identification. It is
better to limit the number of kinds to be recommended than to risk any chance of confusion or
mistaken identity. We would lose no opportunity of
cautioning those who have no general notion of fungi
against making experiments in eating kinds of which
they have no knowledge, or entertain any doubt.

The Parasol mushroom is known and appreciated throughout Europe, and is doubtless one of the first class for the table, with the great advantage that only dense stupidity could confound it with any suspicious species. Dr Bull says of it, "there can be no question but that, when young and quickly grown, it is a delicious fungus. It has a high and delicate flavour without the heavy richness which belongs to the ordinary field mushroom." He adds that he had prevailed on many persons to try it, all, without exception have liked it, and about one third of the number have thought it quite equal and some have proclaimed it superior to the mushroom itself.

BROILED PARASOL MUSHROOM.—Remove the scales and stalks, and broil lightly over a clear fire on both sides for a few minutes ; arrange them on a dish, over fresh made well-divided toast ; sprinkle with pepper and salt, and put a small piece of butter on each ; set before a brisk fire to melt the butter, and serve quickly.

BAKED PARASOL MUSHROOM.—Remove the scales and stalks, and place the caps in layers in a dish ; put a little butter on each, and season with pepper and salt. Cover lightly and bake for twenty minutes or half an hour, according to the number in the dish. Put them on hot toast in a hot dish. Pour the hot sauce over them and serve quickly.

STEWED PARASOL MUSHROOM.—Remove the stalks and scales from young specimens, and throw each one as you do so into a basin of fresh water, slightly acidulated with the juice of a lemon or a little good vinegar. When all are prepared remove them from the water, and put them into a stewpan with a very small piece of fresh butter, sprinkle with white pepper and salt, and add a little lemon juice. Cover up closely, and stew for half-an-hour. Then add a spoonful of flour with sufficient cream, or cream and milk, until the same has the thickness of cream. Season to taste, and stew again gently until all are perfectly tender. Remove all the butter from the surface and serve in a hot dish, garnished with slices of lemon. A little mace, nutmeg, or catsup, may be added, if preferred, but some think that the spice spoils the flavour.

PARASOL SAUCE.—Chop up about half a pint of these agarics, pepper and salt, and add an ounce of butter rolled in flour. Put in a stewpan over a slow fire for a few minutes; add half a pint of milk, or better still, cream, and boil gently, stirring all the time until it is sufficiently thick and smooth. Pour round boiled fowls or rabbits, or any light fricassee.

Beef or veal stock may be used when a brown sauce is required; and some think a little mace or nutmeg, or a few drops of Indian Soy, or a little Harvey sauce, a good addition. The brown sauce is excellent for steaks, cutlets, game, or any kind of râgout.

SCALLOPED PARASOL MUSHROOM.—Mince young

fresh agarics, season with pepper, salt, and a little lemon juice, add a little butter, and stew in a warm oven for ten minutes, then put them in the scallop tin, layer by layer, with fresh bread crumbs moistened with milk, cream, or good gravy; bake for five minutes, and brown well before a quick fire.

PROCERUS PIE.—Cut the fresh agarics in small pieces, and cover the bottom of a pie dish. Pepper, salt, and place on them small shreds of fresh bacon, then put a layer of mashed potatoes, and so fill the dish layer by layer, with a cover of mashed potatoes for the crust. Bake well for half-an-hour, and brown before a quick fire.

PROCERUS OMELETTE.—Mince some young fresh agarics; season with pepper and salt; add butter and set them in the oven whilst you whisk well the whites and yolks of half a dozen eggs; then put two ounces of butter into the frying pan, and heat until it begins to brown; having again well whisked up the eggs, with three tablespoonfuls of the prepared agarics and a little milk, pour it lightly into the boiling butter; stir one way, and fry on one side only for five or six minutes; drain it from the fat; roll it up and serve quickly on a hot well covered dish.

POTTED PROCERUS.—Remove the scales and stalks from young fresh specimens; sprinkle with pepper and salt, and set aside for three or four hours, then place them in a stewpan with the liquor that will have exuded, and stew until dry; next fry in butter for a few minutes; put them into small jars, and when cold pour in as much butter melted as will just cover them; when again cold pour on a little melted suet and tie down with bladder. When required for use soak them for two or three hours in a little warm milk and water, and stew with milk, cream, or stock, and use in any way that may be required.

ESSENCE OF PROCERUS.—Sprinkle young but full grown agarics with salt, and let them stand for six hours. Then beat them well up, and the next day strain off the liquor, and boil very slowly until it is reduced to one half the quantity. This will not keep long, but if one eighth part of good French brandy, or half its quantity of any wine, be added, and bottled carefully, it will then keep for any reasonable time.

PROCERUS KETCHUP.—Take full grown, but not worm-eaten agarics, and place them layer by layer in a deep pan, sprinkling each layer as it is put in with a little salt. The next day stir them well up several times, so as to mash and extract the juice. On the third day strain off the liquor, measure and boil for ten minutes, then to every pint of the liquor add half an ounce of black pepper, a quarter of an ounce of bruised ginger, a blade of mace, a clove or two, and a teaspoonful of mustard seed. Boil again for half an hour, put in two or three bay leaves, and set aside till quite cold. Pass through a strainer and bottle ; cork well and dip the ends in resin ; a very little Chili vinegar is an improvement, and some add a glass of port wine, or strong ale, to every bottle.

The majority of the above are from the " Woolhope Club " receipts.

VIII.—ST GEORGE'S MUSHROOM.

THE only really good spring mushroom, except the Morels is the St George's mushroom (*Agaricus gambosus*), presumably so called because it makes its first appearance about St George's day.

There is a legend accounting for the name, which is current in Hungary, that it was a gift from St George. Readers may please themselves which account they choose to adopt. Some confusion has also prevailed as to the scientific name which Dr Badham gave as *Agaricus prunulus*, and some others have called *Agaricus Georgii*, whereas the veritable *prunulus* and also the true *Georgii* are different species. In France it is called *mouceron* or *mousseron* on account of its growing amongst moss, and from this it has been stated that our name " mushroom," applied generally to another species, has been derived.

The St George's mushroom is a pasture-loving species, and is *not* found in woods. In ordinary cir-

cumstances the cap is about three inches in diameter,
but it will reach four or five, and Dr Badham states
that he has found it six inches across, and weighing
between four and five ounces. He adds that he collected one spring at Keston, in Kent, from ten to
twelve pounds in a single ring, and in the one field
from twenty to twenty-five pounds. From this it will
be seen that it is a gregarious species, many specimens being found growing in company, in the form of
rings, or parts of rings, in the same manner as the fairy-
ring champignon. In some parts a prejudice exists
amongst the farmers against them, on the supposition that they injure the grass crops, and for that
reason they are kicked over and destroyed. A better
plan would be to collect them in a basket, and carry
them home to cook ; but prejudice is blind.

In addition to its being found in fields and
pastures in spring, when agarics are rare, and its
gregarious habit, it has also a strong and peculiar
odour, which is rather oppressive if a large number
are taken into a room. The cap is thick in its flesh,
covered with a dry cuticle, soft to the touch, like a
delicate kid glove, smooth but often cracking when
old. In colour it is usually of a creamy whiteness,
inclined to become yellowish at the top, and not so
regular in form as the ordinary mushroom, but lobed,
and waved at the margin, which is turned in for a
long time, and wholly of a firm substance. When cut
through the flesh is often nearly an inch thick at the

centre. The stem is thick (nearly an inch) and short, of the same colour as the cap, rather thicker at the base, and often contorted, or irregular. The gills are of a watery white, and very numerous, commonly arched, reaching the stem, to which they are attached. The spores also are white. It would be difficult to confound this with any other species, especially when it is remembered that all fungi are rare at the time of its appearance, and if our description is read over carefully, it would be difficult to mistake it at any time, not forgetting the strong odour, its growing in rings, and its white gills and spores. We have never encountered anyone who disliked this mushroom when tasted, but we have heard it objected to as being rather heavy and indigestible for delicate stomachs. Experience, however, has never enabled us to support this charge, and we can only say with Dr Badham, that "it is the most savoury fungus with which we are acquainted."

There are two or three other agarics which have many points in common with the foregoing, from a gastronomic point of view, that we purpose including them here, as the same modes of cooking are applicable to all. The first of these are the Blewits (*Agaricus personatus*), which is a truly autumnal species, sometimes collected as late as November, and seldom appearing at all until October. It loves the grass in open places, such as parks, but not woods and forests. Sowerby has stated that in his time it

was occasionally sold under the name of " Blewits '
in Covent Garden Market, but we have never seen it
exposed for sale in this country. It is more regular
in the shape of its cap than the St George's mushroom,
and similar in size, from two to five or six inches,
smooth, but not viscid, with an oily appearance. In
colour it is most commonly of a dirty white, sometimes greyish, or with a tinge of violet, also thick in
the flesh, and firm, but it imbibes water readily, so
that it is liable to become sodden and dark in wet
weather. The edge is at first turned in, and looks
frosted, or minutely velvety, but this soon disappears.
The stem is from one to three inches long, and about
three quarters of an inch thick, rather swollen at the
base, and stained with lilac, which colour also pene-
trates into the flesh of the stem. The gills are
numerous, rounded behind, and scarcely attached to
the stem, dirty white, now and then tinged with
violet, but the spores are white. It has a strong
odour, but not so powerful as the St George's mushroom, and is equally pleasant to the taste. This is
also a gregarious species, and is said to be fond of
growing in rings, but we have never recognised this
habit although several specimens will generally be
found growing in company. Altogether this fungus
seems to correspond, as a late species, to the St
George's, which is an early one, and they have several
points in common, but there is no suspicion of its
being the same species, indeed this could hardly be

possible. The similarity extends even to the flavour when cooked, although we retain a preference for the former. The Blewits should not be collected for the table when they are water-logged ; since they will hardly give satisfaction in that condition, but when in a good state, they are undoubtedly an excellent esculent.

Another species which seems to have been confounded by earlier writers with "Blewits" under the name of "Blue Caps" is a very common autumnal species amongst dead leaves in woods. Perhaps for this the name of "Bluecaps" might be appropriated (*Agaricus nudus*). It is really a very fine and handsome species, gregarious like the others, but when young of a light violet blue, becoming ruddy with age. In books it is said to be two inches in diameter, but we have seen twenty individuals growing together, not one of which was less than five or six inches. The cap is at first convex, but soon flattened, quite smooth, not viscid, and at last depressed, and almost brick red. It has been called amethyst colour, but there is much more blue in the tone than in amethyst, and it has always a remarkably clean appearance. The stem varies according to the size of the cap, for in the large specimens alluded to it was six or seven inches long, and more than an inch thick, but more commonly it is half those dimensions. In colour the stem is similar to the cap, but perhaps a little paler, with a little white woolliness at the base.

The gills are numerous, and either rounded behind or running down the stem, at first of the same colour as the cap, but becoming ruddy with age. The spores are quite white. For the table we always collect specimens which retain their violet blue colour, and of these we have seen sufficient within an hour to fill a bushel basket. It is, in some places, where there are plenty of dead leaves on the ground, one of the commonest autumnal species. In other places it seems to be comparatively rare. Once recognized and identified it cannot be confounded with any other species, and we have breakfasted upon it daily for a week, without surfeit or inconvenience. It has but a very slight odour, and possesses a more delicate flavour than either of the foregoing.

The St George mushroom has secured for itself in all countries where it is known golden opinions. In some instances this is probably due to the successful intervention of the cook, since fungi, more than aught else, depend much on the efficiency of the cook. If the cooking of fungi has not yet been elevated to the position of a high art, it deserves to be, for the same fungus will please or displease with the merits of the operator. Dr Badham declared this to be the most savoury fungus with which he was acquainted, and justly considered so over almost the whole continent of Europe. Edwin Lees, who was a pronounced mycophagist, was "inclined to give it the highest place as an agaric for the table. There is nothing

about its appearance to displease the most fastidious.
It has an amiable and clean look, grows in pastures
of fresh springing grass, and has an ambrosial smell
—an aroma different from and more pleasant than
the strong catsuppy odour of the common mushroom.
It has a delicate appearance when served up, and
an agreeable taste. Whoever has partaken of it once
wishes to do so again." The Rev. M. J. Berkeley
had always a good word in its favour. He says—
" it is one that a person cannot very well make any
mistake about. It sometimes attains a large size, is
excellent in flavour, and particularly wholesome."
To this might be added the testimony of Mr Worthington Smith, himself an incorrigible fungus-eater,
who remarks that—" few species are more substantial
and delightful for the table. I look upon it with
unusual favour, as one of the rarest delicacies of the
vegetable kingdom." The late Dr Bull said of it,
that "when grown quickly after the rains of early
spring, and before attacked by grubs, it is certainly
an excellent agaric. It has a very delicate flavour,
and is very light and wholesome. When gathered in
dry weather it is more firm in texture, and not so
good in flavour."

After such testimonials, we need only refer to the
methods which have been specially recommended for
its preparation. Dr Badham considered the best
method to be "either to mince, or fricassee it with
any sort of meat, or in a *vol-au-vent*, the flavour of

which it greatly improves ; or, simply prepared with
salt, pepper, and a small piece of bacon, lard, or
butter, to prevent burning, it constitutes of itself an
excellent dish."

The Woolhope Club receipt is to "place some
fresh made toast nicely divided, on a dish and put
the agarics upon it, with a small piece of butter on
each ; then pour on each a teaspoonful of milk or
cream, and add a single clove to the whole dish.
Place an inverted basin over the whole, bake for
twenty minutes, and serve without removing the
basin until it comes to the table, so as to preserve
the heat and the aroma, which, on lifting the cover,
will be diffused through the room."

This is also one of the species which dries readily
when divided into pieces, or sliced, and in this form
retains much of its excellence. A few pieces added
to soups, gravies, or made dishes gives to them a
delicious flavour. To prevent their becoming mouldy
when kept in close tins or bottles, they must be
stored in a perfectly dry place. For this, and all
other dried fungi, it is recommended *not* to exclude
them entirely from the air, as they would be in
bottles or canisters, but to store them in linen or
muslin bags, which allows any contained moisture to
escape, without producing mouldiness, or a musty
flavour.

The modes of cooking are the same in the case
of the blue caps (*Tricholoma nuda*) the Blewits

(*Tricholoma personata*) and St George's mushroom (*Tricholoma gambosa*). They may all be grilled or fried in the same manner as the common mushroom, but we do not think them so well suited for stewing. Perhaps the most successful plan is to place a lump of butter in the frying-pan with a sufficiency of gravy or milk, and a little curry powder, fry for seven or eight minutes, then throw in the sliced agarics, fry gently for ten minutes, and serve up quickly with sippets of toast.

It is also a good method to remove the stems and divide the caps down the centre. Place the pieces in a pie dish with a little pepper and salt, and a small piece of butter on each half. Either tie a paper close over the dish, or cover it closely by other means, and bake gently for about half an hour. Serve in the same dish, which should not be uncovered until placed on the table.

A simpler method is to cut off the stems close, sprinkle pepper and salt over them, and place them in a frying-pan, gills upwards, in the fat after the bacon has been fried, or in default of bacon to place a piece of butter on each cap. Then fry them until thoroughly done, when they will be soft all over, and appetising in odour and taste. They may be served with bacon, or on toast.

IX.—WARTED CAPS.

THERE are a certain number of fungi of the mushroom kind, which are distinguishable from all the
rest, by having raised spots, or warts, or sometimes
patches on the surface of the caps, and at the same
time a more or less distinct membrane sheathing the
base of the stem like a stocking. The explanation
of these appearances is found in the fact, that, in
the young state, whilst the fungus is a mere ball, and
the stem is undeveloped, the whole is enclosed in a
close fitting outer membrane, so that it somewhat
resembles a small egg. As the stem grows, and
lengthens, the outer membrane is torn apart all
round, and the upper portion is carried up, adhering
to the cap, whilst the lower portion remains at the
base of the stem, as a sheath or volva, after the
manner of a boot or stocking. During subsequent
growth of the cap in all directions, and its expansion, the remains of the outer membrane, which was
carried up, adhering closely to it—crack in all directions, and the fragments attached to the cap, become
like whitish patches, or warts, on the surface, in some
cases more divided than in others, sometimes very
closely adhering to the cap, and then small, at other
times loose, and larger, more irregular, and soon falling off.

One of these "warted cap" mushrooms is very common in the early autumn, amongst grass, generally under trees. It is of a dullish lilac tinged with pink, becoming redder with age (*Agaricus rubescens*), and the prominent warts are small, paler, and very numerous, especially on the upper or central portion of the cap, which is two, three, or four inches in diameter. The redness on all parts of the fungus is a dull brick red, and *not* a bright scarlet, or orange. This is a special caution, as there is such a bright coloured species, especially under birch trees, which must be avoided. Returning to the species we were describing, it has a thick stem, four or five inches long, and an inch thick at the swollen base, but attenuated upwards near the top is a broad, pendulous white ring. The gills are white, broad, and do not touch the stem. Very soon the gills and whitish stem show reddish stains, the bottom of the stem especially being darker, and reddish. When cut longitudinally down the stem, the bottom portion of the flesh is stained with red. The volva, or sheath at the base adheres so closely as to be scarcely distinguishable, except for a rough edge like an indistinct ring at the base. The flesh of the cap is white, often with a slight tinge of red, and thick. It is pleasant both in taste and smell, but very soon the stem is perforated, and eaten by larvæ, as it becomes mature. They are in their best condition before the cap is fully expanded, and whilst it is still hemispherical.

This is a good species to serve as an illustration of the origin of the ring, or frill, which surrounds the upper part of the stem in some of the mushrooms. Whilst the cap is still unopened, and represents about two-thirds of a globe, the gills of the under surface will be observed to be covered by a white membrane which reaches from the stem, horizontally, to the edge of the cap. In this stage, if an individual specimen is collected and carried into a warm room, the bottom of the stem placed in a vessel of water, in the course of an hour or two the cap will open out, so as to become flatter, and in doing so the edge recedes from the stem, which causes the membrane to tear away gradually from the edge of the cap, and fall down, like a broad white frill, or ring, towards the stem, the inner edge still remaining attached to the stem. In this way the gills will become exposed. So that the ring is a membrane, which at first covers and protects the gills whilst young, afterwards falling away at the outer edge, but remaining attached by the inner edge to the stem, sometimes it is made up of thin delicate threads, like cobweb, and at other times it is absent or very small.

The true warted mushrooms have all of them a large membranous ring (except in a small and distinct group, in which the ring is absent). It is well worth while taking the trouble to make the acquaintance of the species described above, because when once it is accurately identified, there never need be any fear of mistake, and it is a very common, safe, and useful species.

We may allude here, incidentally, to another species (*Agaricus strobiliformis*) which is unfortunately rare, but equally edible, found on the borders of woods. The cap when young is nearly spherical, but soon expands, reaching a diameter of eight or nine inches. The scales, or warts are large, and not unlike the scales of a fir cone, brownish in the centre, with a white woolly margin, closely adhering to the cap. The stem is six or seven inches long and an inch and a half thick, firm and solid, swollen at the base. The ring is large and pendulous. The gills do not reach the stem, and are rounded behind. The whole fungus is commonly whitish but sometimes pale grey, and there are never any red stains, as in the previous species. To prevent misapprehension it may be added that the gills and spores are white. Hitherto we have only known this species to occur in two or three counties of England, and in those very rarely, so that, large and excellent though it may be, the finding of it must be regarded as a memorable event. One who has eaten it says, "its undisputed esculent qualities are of a high order, and it is to be regretted that its comparative rarity must prevent its being so well known and appreciated as its merits deserve."

It is unnecessary to quote authorities for the excellence and utility of the common warted mushroom, no one disputes it now-a-days, at least among fungus eaters. Generally it has the reputation of being an excellent substitute for the ordinary mushroom, and we know of some who prefer it for its milder flavour. It produces a very good pale ketchup, and being found in most localities in abundance, is available for that purpose, an advantage will be found in its comparative early appearance, since it may always be looked for in July. Only young specimens should be used, or those not attacked by insects. It is shockingly liable to become maggoty.

All methods of cooking available for the mushroom are applicable to this. There is no more delicate and digestible mushroom dish for breakfast than the " warted mushroom," fried with the gills upwards and a piece of butter, with pepper and salt on each, served on toast. It is better to rub off the warts from the cap, as they do not peel easily, and, of course, discard the stems.

There are no special directions for ketchup, as the ordinary method in use for mushroom ketchup is applicable to all species. There must be no disappointment that the ketchup is not black. The flavour must be regarded and not the colour. This is a soft fleshy fungus and will not submit to be dried satisfactorily for subsequent use, indeed it is very difficult to dry it in the air at all without becoming infested with larvæ. We have been informed that the young buttons will pickle well, but of this we have no experience.

Before closing this chapter we may advert to another common fungus, which has a warted cap, and a volvate, or booted, base to the stem but without a ring. Its scientific name signifies "sheathed mushroom" (*Agaricus vaginatus*). The cap is rounded above, longer than hemispherical, from an inch and a half to three inches across, sometimes four inches when expanded, white, mouse-coloured, or brownish, with fragments of the outer membrane loosely adhering to the surface, but soon washed away. The margin is thin, and marked with parallel depressed lines. This is often a useful feature for its determination. The stem is white and slender, gradually attenuated upwards, about six or seven inches long, blunt at the base, but not bulbous, and sheathed with a large, loose ragged volva, or stocking. The gills are snowy white, not reaching to the stem, and the spores are also white.

Careful attention to some of these features in particular, will obviate mistakes. The spots, or irregular fragments, adhering to the cap, and the loose ragged stocking at the base of the stem, which latter is *not* bulbous, together with the parallel lines on the edge of the cap, should be sufficient distinctions to recognise this species anywhere. The cap is comparatively thin in its flesh, and it is rather delicate and fragile. The white variety always has the preference for cooking but the mouse-coloured forms are most common. It is found on the ground in woods, during the autumn, but it is rather solitary in its habits. The only method we have adopted for cooking is that recommended for some other delicate species, after adding pepper, salt and butter, to place them in a plate or dish, cover with an inverted basin and place in an oven for ten minutes. Serve on sippets of toast.

X.—DUSKY CAPS.

MOST people have favourites in food, as well as in everything else, and we have our favourite mushrooms, which we always collect in preference to any others. One of these is the parasol mushroom, but later than that, and when all the parasols are closed for the winter, we direct our special attention to the dusky caps, or cloudy mushroom (*Agaricus nebularis*) which flourishes to the end of November, and we have eaten it as late as the 12th of December, at which period edible fungi are rare. It is neither a small nor a solitary species, since in some years, in a favoured spot, we have seen sufficient within an hour to fill a wheelbarrow. Twenty or thirty-five specimens growing amongst the same heap of dead leaves, nearly covered and sheltered from the frost.

In this species the cap is from two and a half to six inches in diameter, convex at first, but soon flattened,

but not depressed. The margin is at first strongly
curved inwards, but at length is flattened out, and,
when old, with a tendency to bend outwards ; it is quite
smooth, a little streaky, and viscid, so that leaves will
adhere to it. Its usual colour is a cloudy grey,
darker at the centre, and pale at the edge; sometimes
it is a creamy or dirty white, with a greyish centre,
but this is chiefly in late grown specimens. There is
often a kind of glaucous bloom on the caps, like the
" bloom " of a plum. The flesh is very thick, especially about the centre, and gradually attenuated
towards the margin, white and unchangeable. The
stem is from two to four inches long, and rarely six,
from half an inch to upwards of an inch thick, nearly
equal, or a little thickened below, adhering at the
base by a floccose white mycelium, dirty white, and
longitudinally striate, spongy within but seldom
becoming hollow. The gills are rather narrow for the
size of the cap, and attenuated behind, so as to run a
little way down the stem, they are numerous and close,
and creamy white. The spores are small and white.
The odour is rather strong and fungoid ; Dr Badham
says it is like curd cheese, whilst others content themselves with describing it as strong. When raw the
flavour is mild. As already suggested, its favourite
place of growth is amongst dead leaves. In large
gardens it is the custom to sweep up the fallen leaves
in the autumn, and deposit them in a heap, in a quiet
corner to rot. On such heaps we have invariably

found this mushroom in October or November. In woods, where the leaves drift into a ditch or hollow, the "dusky caps" will be found, often partly obscured by the leaves. If the stems are cut off close to the gills when gathered a goodly number of the flat caps can be stowed away in a small compass, which is an advantage, since, when found, it is so gregarious in habit that a plentiful supply may be reckoned upon.

This is known and eaten upon the Continent, but, in some countries, not so well as it deserves, and we have observed in one volume, which is usually trustworthy, it is stated that this species is suspicious, although eaten in England. Such an observation never could have been made by any person who had a practical knowledge of its qualities. In Italy it is not in general request, and according to all accounts it must be rather rare in that country, although common enough in Northern Europe. Other writers fear that it is rather indigestible, whilst Dr Badham says, "the flesh is perhaps lighter of digestion than that of any other."

This fungus has a flavour which at once suggests the common mushroom, but milder, which to some tastes would seem preferable. In many cases it is not easy to compare the flavour, since it is so dissimilar to the "mushroom," and such species are often disappointing to inexperienced fungus-eaters since they know of but one flavour, and to this they expect all others to conform ; it is only after they have learnt that nearly every kind of edible fungus has its own characteristic flavour, that they reconsider and often reverse their verdict.

In cooking the "dusky caps" it is sufficient to wipe them, since they do not grow in contact with the soil, and hence are not liable to be gritty. The cuticle of the cap is not separable easily, and need not be denuded. When the stems are rejected the caps may be put in a stewpan with butter, salt and pepper, or a spoonful of cream ; or they may be fried with the bacon for breakfast. Any treatment suitable for the common mushroom will be applicable, but it is a tender species and requires but a short time in cooking. Dr Badham says it may be delicately fried with bread crumbs, or stewed in white sauce. Some writers have indulged in a little sly sarcasm at the recommendation to use gravy, or stock, or such like additions in cooking fungi, either, as they observe, to conceal the flavour, where it is not quite agreeable, or to impart a flavour where there is none. Those critics had forgotten that mushrooms, of no kind, are required to be crisp, and that the liquid added to them is intended to furnish moisture, and keep them tender ; but should it happen to be an affair of conscience, it may soothe them to learn that they may substitute water, or milk, or cream, for gravy or sauce, and they might venture on bacon fat, beef dripping, or salad oil, if these are more to their taste than butter.

We are induced to add to this chapter some features
by which two or three other good species may be recognized, which are akin to "dusky caps." The large
funnel mushrooms, with a cap so deeply sunk in the
centre that it resembles a funnel, are too rare to require more than a passing reference. The "giant
mushroom" nearly a foot in diameter (*Agaricus
giganteus*) and the "large funnel" which is not so
broad (*Agaricus maximus*) but nearly a foot in height,
are excellent food, but they occur so seldom as to
amount almost to phenomena. One large funnel
shaped mushroom (*Agaricus geotropus*) is rather more
common, but perhaps local, and deserves mention.
During last autumn (1890) when fungi of all kinds have
been exceptionally scarce, we saw ten or twelve fine
specimens brought in from a day's excursion. The cap
is creamy white, or pale tan colour, four or five inches
broad, deeply depressed, like a funnel, smooth, soft
and fleshy. Stem six inches long, so that with the
rising cap the whole fungus would attain to nine
inches ; this solid stem tapering upwards from a base
an inch-and-a-half thick, and more or less fibrous.
The gills numerous and crowded, running down the
stem, white at first, and then almost of the colour
of the cap. The flesh is thick, nearly an inch in
large specimens, sweet and nutty to the taste, and a
slight mealy odour. It grows in woods or on their
borders, several specimens together, or forming part
of a ring. This is equal to the dusky caps as an

esculent, but hardly the same in flavour. No one who has once partaken of it would refuse to do so again. It may be prepared for the table in the same manner as the foregoing species.

There is a smaller mushroom (*Agaricus infundibuliformis*) almost a miniature of *geotropus*, common in woods everywhere, about two inches broad and high, which is most delicate and delicious served on toast.

XI.—THE FAIRY RING CHAMPIGNON.

IT would be a fallacy to suppose because this is called the " Fairy Ring Champignon " that it is the only fungus which delights in fairy rings, whereas there are several distinct species which possess this proclivity. Still, it is this (*Marasmius oreades*) ·and no other, to which the name of Fairy ring mushroom is exclusively applied. It is assumed to be this which is dedicated to—

> " The nimble elves
> That do by moonshine green sour ringlets make
> Whereof the ewe bites not ; whose pastime 'tis
> To make these midnight mushrooms."

Familiar though they are to those whose home is in the country, many of those who dwell in cities have but a vague notion about fairy rings. For their

edification we may quote a very succinct description—
" Fairy rings consist, generally speaking, of circles, or
parts of circles of grass, of a darker colour, and more
luxuriant growth than the surrounding herbage, the
outer edge of the circle being well defined, while the
colour and stature of the grass diminish and fade so
gradually inwards, that it is difficult to determine the
exact limit of the ring towards the centre. Very
commonly there is to be observed an outer and contiguous ring, much narrower than the inner, and of
which the grass is either short and weak, or faded
and brown, remarkably contrasting with the vivid
green of the inner ring : on this brown ring, or just
upon its margin, fungi are found. The duration of
fairy rings varies much : some disappear in a few
weeks, others endure for years. A severe winter
will obliterate the external traces of a ring, and
prevent the usual crop of fungi appearing upon it at
the proper season ; but such rings often reappear, and
are thus considered to have been suddenly formed.
During the whole course of their appearance the
rings increase in diameter, spreading outwards from
the centre, the faded brown circle becoming rank
with green and copious grass, and a fresh outer circle
being formed of dead or feeble blades of grass. The
rate of increase is various, some enlarging their diameter a few inches in the year, others as many feet.
The circles frequently meet in the course of this
gradual enlargement. In such cases the point of

contact becomes obliterated ; and when this contact
occurs between the margin of several such rings, the
obliteration of the parts which meet leaves a variety
of segments 'of circles upon the turf, which, pursuing
an independent course, and some increasing more
rapidly than others, present eventually an unaccount-
able irregularity, and, as it were, patchwork of greener
and paler, stronger and weaker, portions of turf.
When the turf is cut through such a ring at two
contiguous points, so that a breadth is taken up from
the inner rank green, through the faded breadth, to
the outer ordinary state, the soil of the faded ring is
always found drier and of a paler colour than the
adjoining parts, and abundantly impregnated with
mycelium.   Indeed, a careful examination will show
that the faded and impoverished condition of the turf
of the outer ring is due to the close investment of the
roots by the mycelium of the fungi which occupy the
ring.   The dimensions of the rings vary from 3 feet
to 300 feet in diameter ; they are at times very
irregular in form, an accident arising either from the
nature of the soil, and the obstacles which they meet
with in their circumferential expansion, or from more
than one ring coalescing, and producing an outline of
undulating curves."

But what of the cause and origin of these rings ?
Some curious theories have from time to time been
advanced, and subsided into oblivion.   Amongst the
least probable is one which attributed the agency to

moles, which loosened the soil and caused a more fertile growth. Others have attributed them to lightning, and others again to subterranean vapours ; but the most feasible theory is that which is set forth by the Rev. M. J. Berkeley, in the following words : " These rings are sometimes of very ancient date, and attain enormous dimensions, so as to be distinctly visible on a hill side from a considerable distance. It is believed that they originate from a single fungus whose growth renders the soil immediately beneath unfit for its reproduction. The spawn, however spreads all around, and in the second year produces a crop whose spawn spreads again, the soil behind forbidding its return in that direction. Thus the circle is continually increased, and extends indefinitely till some cause intervenes to destroy it. If the spawn did not spread on all sides at first, an arc of a circle only is produced. The manure arising from the dead fungi of the former years makes the grass peculiarly vigorous round, so as to render the circle visible even when there is no external appearance of the fungus, and the contrast is often the stronger from that behind being killed by the old spawn. This mode of growth is far more common than is supposed, and may be observed constantly in our woods where the spawn can spread only in the soil, or amongst the leaves and decaying fragments which cover it." *

* " Outlines of British Fungology," p. 41.

The fungus which is commonly known as the "fairy ring champignon" (*Marasmius oreades*) is a small, dry looking mushroom, seldom much more than one inch in diameter, and of a warm buff colour, paler when dry. The cap is convex, with a slight depression round the broad central umbo or boss, quite smooth, without any lines or scales ; as it becomes old it is rather flattened. The stem is of equal thickness throughout, whitish, from the size of a straw to that of a clay-pipe stem. The gills are broad, and distant from each other, quite white, or creamy white, or with the slightest tinge of yellow, reaching the stem. The substance is tough and elastic, not brittle, and it dries very readily, never melting. After having been dried, if placed in water it will reassume its former size and shape. This peculiar dry substance and power of reviving is the feature whereby a *Marasmius* may be distinguished from an agaric. It would be folly to seek this species in woods, as it grows in the open, in pastures, lawns, &c., and the species found in woods, which resemble it somewhat in appearance, are not good eating. We have known persons to confound dark brown, and other dark coloured species, with the champignon, simply on account of their gregarious habit. This is absurd, because the true species is always light coloured, even when soaked with moisture, and the gills are nearly white, with white spores. The features which distinguish this from similar species are so permanent

F

and well marked that we cannot comprehend how mistakes so egregious could have been made. Above all things, let it be certain that the spores and gills are white; that the cap is perfectly dry, and not in the least viscid; that the gills are distant apart, so that you may look down between them; and that the whole substance is tough, elastic, and flexible as compared with the agarics. It is possible to carry them home loose in the coat pocket without breaking them, especially in dry weather, and they should be sought after in summer or early autumn. In September, certainly in October, none will be found.

Without repeating all the encomiums that have been passed on the "fairy ring champignon," we will be content with one, which may be accepted as a type of the rest. "It should be stewed with pepper and butter, and then it makes an agreeable condiment. It is also to be recommended for pickling. It might be used as an ingredient in soups all through the year, as its tough nature allows it to be strung up in quantities like onions. This is a very delicious agaric beyond question; and the abundance in which it everywhere grows makes it a very valuable one. The only drawback is its tendency to toughness, which is, however, easily to be surmounted by proper cooking."

The juice of this mushroom, obtained in the same manner as ketchup is made, is strongly recommended, especially when fresh. The quantity obtainable is small, as this is a dry fungus, but the flavour is delicate, although not by any means strong, and unlike ketchup.

CHAMPIGNON POWDER is a good form for winter use. Put the champignons in a stewpan with a little mace and a few cloves, and a sprinkling of white pepper. Simmer and shake constantly to prevent burning, until any liquor that may exude is dried up again. Dry thoroughly in a warm oven until they will easily powder. Put the dried fungi, or the powder, into wide-mouthed bottles, and store in a dry place.

PICKLED CHAMPIGNONS are prepared as follows. Collect fresh buttons of the fairy ring champignon and use them at once. Cut off the stems quite close and throw each one, as you do it, into a basin of water in which a spoonful of salt has been dissolved. Drain them from it quickly afterwards, and lay them on a soft cloth to dry. For each quart of buttons thus prepared take nearly a quart of pale white wine vinegar, and add to it a heaped teaspoonful of salt, half an ounce of whole white pepper, an ounce of ginger bruised, two large blades of mace, and a fourth of a salt spoon of cayenne pepper, tied in a small piece of muslin. When this pickle boils throw in the champignons and boil them in it over a clear fire, moderately fast, from six to nine minutes. When tolerably tender put them into warm, wide-mouthed bottles, and divide the spice equally amongst them ;

when perfectly cold cork well, or tie skins and paper over them. Store in a dry place, and keep out the frost.

For ordinary use the fresh champignons may be cut in small pieces, and seasoned. In this state it may be added to stews, hashes, or fried meats, but it should be added only a few minutes before serving.

XII.—MILKY MUSHROOMS.

A LITTLE experience in collecting fungi will soon convince the student that there are important differences, such as he had scarcely expected to find, and some of them so striking as to cause him to marvel that they should for so long have escaped his observation. One of these is the fact that some of the individuals with the external, and superficial, features of agarics, with cap, stem, and gills, should contain within them a profusion of white, or coloured milk, which oozes out in drops whenever the fungus is wounded. From this circumstance the section, or, as botanists term it, the *genus*, has a special name, and is called *Lactarius*, or milky mushrooms. In some instances the milk is sweet and pleasant to the taste, in others it is hot and peppery, causing the lips to tingle. All are found growing on the ground, mostly in woods, and a few are recommended as articles of food. One species which is esteemed on the continent, where it is more common than with us, attains a considerable size, although not the largest of the milky mushrooms. It is of an orange brown colour (*Lactarius volemus*), with a cap about four inches broad, depressed in the centre, smooth and rather polished, thick in the flesh, which is readily seen by cutting through the cap, and then the sweet white milk will exude, and fall in drops to the ground. The stem is more than three inches long, sometimes four or five, and nearly an inch thick, a little tapering towards the base, rather paler than the centre of the cap, which is darkest, and rather a spongy flesh. The gills are numerous, reaching the stem, and of an ochre colour at first, becoming darker, especially when touched. The spores are white. Like its relatives in this section, it grows on the ground in woods, but is too rare to be of much interest as an esculent. In some seasons we have seen two or three individuals, but more often none at all.

Much more common, and smaller, is the sweet milk mushroom (*Lactarius subdulcis*); indeed this is quite a common species everywhere, but it is not of much account as an esculent, especially as it makes its appearance at a time when better species are to be had. Nearly all the description we have given above of the larger species will apply to this, except that it is smaller and more of a dark cinnamon in

colour, with a reddish tinge, and the gills are darker,
and rather rufous. The milk is white and mild to
the taste. There is an opaque dryness in the appearance of this fungus when it is not overcharged with
moisture by the wetness of the season, which will distinguish it also from small specimens of *Lactarius
volemus.* There is often found growing in company
with it, in the same sort of situations in woods, a
smaller species, of much brighter colour, but always
small (*Lactarius mitissimus*). It is a very mild
species, as its name indicates, and preferable to
subdulcis when cooked. This little milk mushroom
is often about an inch across the pileus, occasionally
double that size, and of an orange colour, with a faint
mixture of brown, but it has no zones, or concentric
bands of a darker colour; the stem is about as long
as the diameter of the cap, and paler, as are also the
numerous gills. There is hardly any very appreciable odour in these three species, and all have a
plentiful supply of sweet white milk, which does not
change colour on exposure to the air. It sometimes
seems a little difficult to draw the line of separation
between these latter two species, for small bright
coloured individuals of *Lactarius subdulcis* are very
like *Lactarius mitissimus.*

After all, the most celebrated is the Orange milk
mushroom (*Lactarius deliciosus*). Even the name
declares it to be one of the most delicious of fungi.
Thus much is assumed by the name, although there

may be heretics who contend for precedence on be-
half of two or three other kinds of fungi, for which
names do not profess so much. Taking for granted
that this is a delicious mushroom, it must always be
sought after under fir trees. It will be waste of time
to hunt for it anywhere else. Fortunately, it grows
in company, and when one has been found it is
probable that twenty will follow. September is the
most favourable month, and the first week in October
is usually too late, except for two or three belated
individuals. The cap is three or four inches in diameter, of a dull reddish orange colour, dimpled or
depressed a little in the centre, with the edge turned
in at first, and for a long time afterwards. The cap
is zoned with concentric bands of brighter colour, but
is liable to be discoloured, because, wherever touched,
or kicked, or bruised, it becomes of a dull green.
The stem is always short, so that the cap grows very
near to the ground ; sometimes scarcely more than
an inch long, and a little attenuated downwards.
The gills are not very close together, and arched so
that they run a little way down the stem, a little paler
than the cap. The most noteworthy feature is that
the milk is orange at first, and turns green by exposure to the air. It is this which causes the decol-
ouration of the cap when bruised. As there is no
other fungus which has an orange milk changing to
green, there is no danger of confusion. When cut
through the cap and stem its identity will at once be

established by the oozing of the orange milk, and even whilst held in the hand that orange will gradually become of a dirty green.

The whole substance of this mushroom is firm and compact to the touch, cutting like an apple or pear, but it has not an attractive appearance on account of the livid green stains.

We cannot close these observations on the milky mushrooms without one or two remarks upon the strictures which some have expressed. In one book before us it is stated that "The milk fungi are suspicious as a group ; this is the only one we can at all recommend." Against this sweeping condemnation we have already described three other species, and we might add three more which are named in our list, but we will rest content with a hint that it is not advisable to give a dog a bad name without sufficient cause.

There is a large white milk mushroom, common in woods, with a cap six or eight inches in diameter (*Lactarius piperatus*), and rather a peppery white milk. In this country it has been condemned by all authors, one after the other, as poisonous, or at the best very suspicious. And yet this same fungus, which is ready of determination, is eaten on the Continent, and Dr Curtis wrote to the Rev. M. J. Berkeley that he had constantly eaten it in the United States, and considered it excellent. We are not prepared to recommend it without first eat-

ing it ourselves, but the evidence is very strong that
this suspicion is one of our insular prejudices.

Another of the milk mushrooms which is less
common (*Lactarius controversus*) equals the last in
size, is also white, but becomes stained, very often,
with dark red, and has flesh coloured gills. This,
again, has always been held suspicious, but although
the white milk is acrid or peppery, this is dispersed
by cooking, and it may be eaten without inconvenience. All we desire, at this time, to infer from
this is that the number of poisonous or disagreeable
fungi is less than has been suspected. There are a
few undoubtedly dangerous, but their number will
bear no comparison with the number of those that
are innocuous. We have always cautioned persons
against making experiments, and do so still, but it is
possible to cherish unreasonable suspicions.

There is a diversity of opinion as to the estimation
in which the orange milk mushroom should be held
as an esculent. Some will not hesitate to endorse the
opinion of Sir J. E. Smith, that "it is the most
delicious mushroom known;" whilst others will
contend that it has been much overrated. Berkeley
writes of it thus—" Dr Badham stayed with me once,
and we had all sorts of things cooked. At last we
got *Lactarius deliciosus*, and my cook said she was
sure if we ate it we should be poisoned, and she
absolutely refused to cook it. It is one which grows
in very great abundance in fir woods occasionally;

and I can positively state myself, having partaken of it, that it is most excellent." Mr Edwin Lees, who was really an epicure, gives it a very good character.

"The rich gravy it produces is its chief characteristic, and hence it commends itself to make a rich gravy sauce, or as an ingredient in soups. It requires delicate cooking, for though fleshy it becomes tough if kept on the fire till all the juice is exuded. Baking is perhaps the best process for it to pass through. It should be dressed when fresh and pulpy." Served at the annual Woolhope dinners, it has always given satisfaction. The pie-dish method of cooking is said to suit it best, as it is firm and crisp in substance. Only sound specimens should be used. These should be reduced by cutting to a uniform bulk. Place the pieces in a pie-dish, with a little pepper and salt, and a small piece of butter on every slice. Cover the dish, or tie it over with paper, and bake gently for three quarters of an hour. Serve in the same hot dish, and do not uncover till it is placed on the table.

This *Lactarius* may also be cut in slices and fried with butter, or bacon, or gravy, and served hot with sippets of toast.

Some enthusiasts strongly recommend *Deliciosus* pie, which is made in the following manner. Pepper and salt the slices of fungus, and place them in layers, with thin slices of fresh bacon, until a small pie-dish is full; cover with a crust of pastry or mashed potatoes, and bake gently for three quarters of an hour. If potatoes are used as a crust, it should be browned nicely before a quick fire.

The same mode of procedure in cooking would doubtless serve with other species of milk agaric, although we have only tried the frying. If only two or three specimens of *Lactarius* are available for the purpose, we have found it answer very well to cut off the stems, and place the caps, gills upwards, on a plate, put a piece of butter and a little salt and pepper on each, cover closely with an inverted basin, and place them in an oven for at least half an hour.

XIII.—THE HEDGEHOG MUSHROOM.

THERE is no safe way of passing through a work of this kind without some allusion to technical distinctions, or as we might state it, without some recognition of the correlation of scientific facts. Although we are desirous of keeping the technicalities of science as much in the background as possible, yet sound definitions should underlie even popular treatises. No further apology therefore is needed for pointing out at once the essential differences which separate fungi of the type now to be described from the agarics and *Boleti*. In the case of the agarics it has been intimated that the first essential is the possession of parallel plates, or gills, on the under-surface of the cap, which constitute the reproductive element. In the *Boleti* the gills are no longer present, but are replaced by tubes which serve the same purpose. And now, with the *Hydnei* or spine bearing tribe, we have the gills or tubes alike absent, but their place is supplied by projecting spines or teeth.

A good illustration will be found in the common Hedgehog Mushroom (*Hydnum repandum*), which may serve first for a short botanical lesson, and afterwards as a dish for the breakfast table. This fungus is sufficiently common in woods in the autumn to be found by anyone who seeks it. The cap re-sembles somewhat an ordinary mushroom, but is more irregular in shape, seldom round, and of a warm cream colour, not unlike the top of a sponge cake. It is about three or four inches across, seldom even, but with irregular knobs or protuberances, and never shining or sticky. Owing to the shortness of the stem the cap is always close to the ground. If we gather one of these, and turn it over, it will be seen that the under surface is covered with closely packed spines, of the same colour as the surface of the cap.

These spines occupy the place, and serve the purpose of gills. This is the scientific distinction between the agarics and the hydnums, and the sum total of our botanical demonstration. In our common hedgehog mushroom the stem is short and thick, often deformed and distorted. Not unusually two

individuals will be found either with caps or stems
grown together, so that they are not symmetrical.
The spines also clothe the upper part of the stem
where it spreads into the cap. The taste of the fresh
fungus is rather warm and peppery, so much so that
thin slices may be added to a sandwich, being placed
on the top of the meat in place of mustard, but having more of the flavour of horseradish. Even when
cooked there still remains a little pungency, but not
more than is pleasant. A basket may soon be filled
with this mushroom in the season, for it is thick and
fleshy, and if one specimen is discovered there will
probably be a dozen more close by. Being of a dry
texture it may be sliced and dried for use in the
winter, but in this case it must always be steeped in
warm water before it is used, or it will be tough.

There is another species of nearly the same size
found in mountain pine woods (*Hydnum imbricatum*),
but it is very rare in England, and only occasional in
Scotland. The cap is brown and scaly, the spines
are greyish white. This does not appear to be an
uncommon species in the north of Europe, but with
us the cream coloured species takes its place, whilst
this in some parts of northern Europe, is rather
scarce. According to all accounts it is in no way
superior as an esculent to our common species.
Other kinds with a central stem are found occasionally, but rarely in the south, and these have a tough
leathery substance so as to be out of the question as

esculents. It is a little remarkable that we have no knowledge of a single species of the fleshy kind which has the reputation of being poisonous.

Finally, there are three species which grow upon trees, which have all been found, at one time or other, in this country, but their appearances are almost historical events, so that they have come to be regarded as great rarities, too valuable for consumption.

The cauliflower spiny cap (*Hydnum coralloides*) has somewhat the appearance of a cauliflower when young, forming a large dense mass, with a very much branched stem, and the ultimate branches thin, bearing on one side only, so that no caps are produced. Looked upon as it grows it appears only as a mass of spines.

Another is the "tree hedgehog" (*Hydnum erinaceum*) which forms a tough fleshy mass, six or eight inches long, and half as broad. The outer surface is covered with very long, drooping spines. It is not unlike a hedgehog in size and form, but white at first, and afterwards yellowish, and has been found generally on oak or beech trunks.

The third species, "Medusa's head" (*Hydnum caput medusæ*), has somewhat the form of the last and is at first snowy white, becoming greyish. The spines are also very long and slender. However, it is unnecessary to give any lengthened description of these rarities, since it is hardly probable that they will gladden the eyes of our readers, and, if so, all have the reputation of being edible.

There is only one final member of this group which, though small, is much more common. This is the "jelly hedgehog" (*Tremellodon gelatinosum*), found on old fir trunks. It is almost of the consistence of jelly, of a brownish colour, with paler spines. The peculiarity in this as an edible fungus, on the authority of the French, is that it should be eaten raw, with wine, in the same manner as a jelly, and will serve the same purpose. It is the only fungus of which we have ever heard that is capable of such an application, and even of this we must confess to being without experience.

The conflicting opinions which have been expressed on the merits of the hedgehog mushroom have doubtless depended more than in any other species upon the cook. Berkeley says truly of it that it is a most excellent fungus, but requires a little caution in preparation for the table. It should be previously steeped in hot water and well drained in a cloth ; in which case there is certainly not a more excellent fungus than it is. Undoubtedly it is a dense and dry fungus, so that in whatever way it may be cooked it should be done slowly, at a low temperature, until it is tender, and with plenty of stock or white sauce to supply its deficiency in moisture. There is a little pungency, not at all disagreeable, but very evident in all results, which is one of its characteristics. Thin slices of the raw fungus when inserted in a sandwich in place of mustard is a very agreeable change, not uncommonly resorted to by fungus hunters " on foray days."

A French method is to slice the fungi and steep them for twenty minutes in warm water ; after being well drained they are placed in a pan with butter, pepper, salt, and parsley, with beef gravy or white sauce, and allowed to simmer for an hour.   Everyone recommends stewing as the best method for *Hydnum*, and one writer says that when cut up in pieces about the size of a bean, and stewed in white sauce, it will almost pass as oyster sauce.

A very fine kind of dark coloured hedgehog mush-room, with a cap often six inches in diameter, is highly esteemed in Japan, either fresh or dried, in which latter case they are often dried whole in a current of air, and preserved for winter use.

XIV.—SWEETBREAD MUSHROOMS.

It has always been an article of faith with us that the group of mushrooms which possess pink or salmon coloured spores is the most suspicious of all the sections of agarics ; that some of them are un-doubtedly poisonous and others cause considerable inconvenience when eaten by mistake.   Relying upon

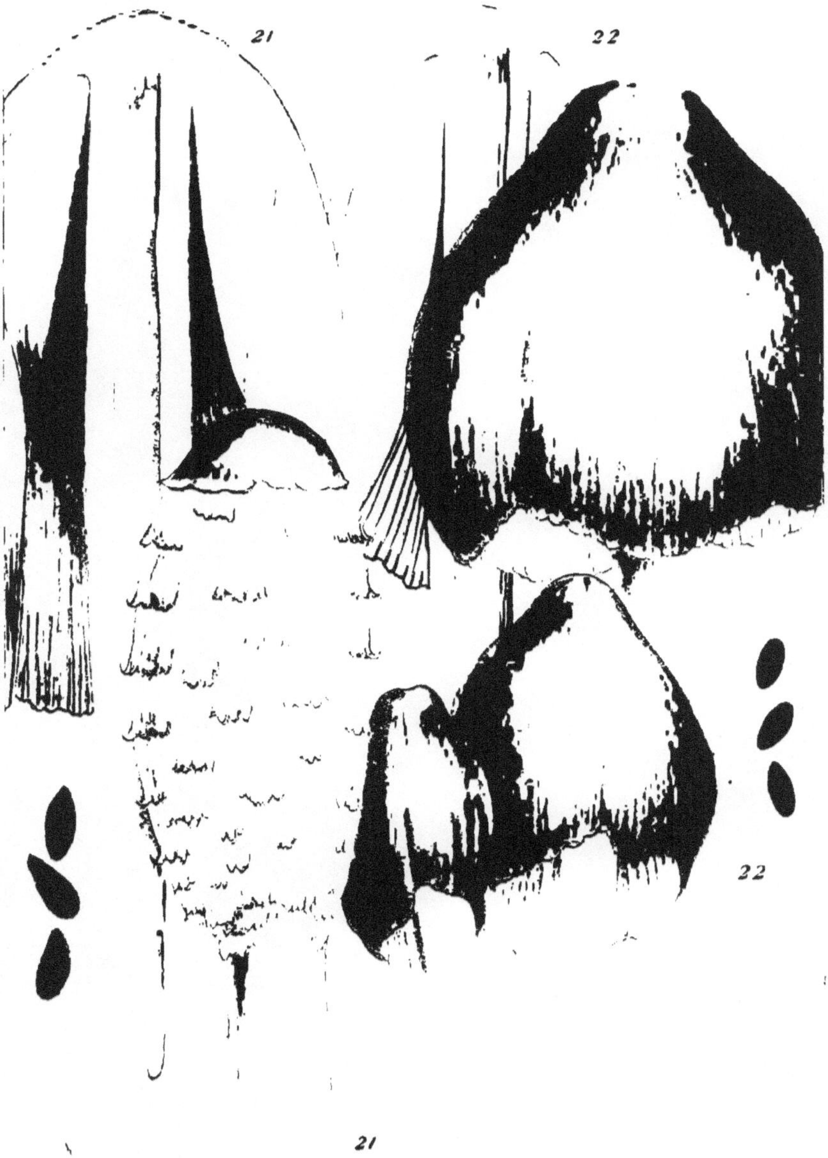

21

22

22

21

this faith, it has always been felt to be incumbent upon us to utter a note of warning whenever the subject would justify it. Even now, with maturer experience, we are not disposed to withdraw our suspicions, or relax our warnings. It is not that the deleterious properties reside in the colour of the spores, which we do not assume, but the presence of other elements in the fungi themselves, exhibited in some instances by rapid putrefaction, and in many by a strong nitrous odour, in which the danger lies. The colour of the spores alone is not a safe basis for any conclusion, since some of those with white spores are amongst the most virulent ; and yet we do not condemn white-spored agarics in a mass. In this instance we simply take advantage of one feature as a simple means of indicating a suspicious group, instead of resorting to scientific names indicating special genera. Experience has shown that certain groups appear to be, for some occult reason, more generally injurious than others, with but a few solitary exceptions, and we take advantage of any recognisable feature which will indicate that group ; and in this case the most available one is the colour of the spores.

Notwithstanding this general character of the pink spored agarics, we have in two or three well defined species remarkable exceptions to the rule, and it is to these that the present chapter is devoted. This only proves that the colour of the spores is not the disturbing element, but it does not militate against the conclusion that, as a general rule, pink spored species should not be experimented upon without positive knowledge of their properties.

Some people think that the fungi we designate as two species are in reality only two forms of the same species, but that is a question which it would be out of place to discuss here. Both are supposed to have a similar resemblance to sweetbreads when prepared for the table, and hence the name. The most delicate of the two is the orcella, or true vegetable sweetbread (*Agaricus orcella*), which has a thin, irregular cap two or three inches in diameter, of an ivory whiteness, or sometimes with a greyish tinge, especially at the centre. There is a peculiar satiny lustre, which is more pronounced when the weather is dry. The cap soon becomes depressed and concave, with the margin lobed or undulated, so as often to present a very irregular and unsymmetrical appearance. In moist weather the surface becomes a little sticky, so as to adhere to the fingers, but it is always soft and smooth. The stem is short and white, decreasing downwards, solid within, sometimes placed in the centre, and sometimes towards one side of the cap. The gills are numerous and closely crowded, running down the stem, and attenuated towards both ends. At first they are nearly white, then they become of a pale greyish pink, and when old pass into a peculiar pale lightish brown. For a long time the gills retain their

dirty white colour, and it has all the appearance of a
white spored species. When cut in section the flesh
is white and unchangeable. The odour is described
as that of fresh meal, but some persons fancy a
resemblance, or suggestion, of cucumber ; at any rate
it is always distinct and recognisable. It grows
amongst grass in woods, or their borders, from June
to September, with a preference for open places.

The other has been called for distinction the " plum
mushroom " (*Agaricus prunulus*), and when compared
together will be found to be the more regular shaped
and fleshy of the two. The cap under ordinary
circumstances is from two to three inches broad, but
it will attain as much as five inches, at first convex,
and afterwards flattened, but ultimately depressed in
the centre ; the margin is often wavy and irregular
when mature. It is white, like the other, with a tinge
of grey, with a sort of bloom, or frostiness on the
surface, resembling the "bloom" on a plum. The
stem is rather short, from an inch and more long, and
half an inch in thickness, white, and a little woolly at
the base. The gills, in all essentials, are the same as
in the other species, of the same peculiar colour, for
a long time whitish, and running down the stem.
The flesh also is solid, white, and unchangeable. The
odour of new meal is evidently somewhat stronger
and more overpowering than in the former species.
It grows also amongst grass in woods, preferring
shady places more than its companion, and is more

gregarious in its habits, a number of individuals
being often found together, occasionally in the form
of a ring.

To avoid possible error in reference, it may be
intimated that the species mentioned by Dr Badham
under the name of *Agaricus prunulus* is not the
present species, but the St George's mushroom. In
that work the two are confounded, or united, which
we have described above, and he says of them
collectively—" It is a very delicate mushroom." An
enthusiastic lady, writing of the species, says—" No
mushroom is more in harmony with the idea of fairy
rings and merry woodland sprites than this. Fre-
quenting the precincts of the forests of long ago, it
flourishes in the very localities where imagination
might suppose the tiny people would linger, and what
so suitable for their midnight fetes as the alabaster
tables covered with silky white damask, which the
caps of the moucerons present ? " Only that this is *not*
the " mouceron," which again is the St George's
mushroom, another case of confusion of names.

We are not concerned much with the differences
between *Orcella* and *Prunulus*, and whether they are
forms of one species, or whether they are two distinct
species. It is sufficient that they are both very good to
eat. One writer who considered them distinct, says
that " *Orcella* is a smaller and more delicate fungus
than *Prunulus*. It is thinner and less fleshy, more
undulated at the margin, and has a lighter and more

agreeable odour. *Orcella* grows in more open glades than *Prunulus*, it is usually much whiter in colour, sometimes in high situations, white, and glazed as egg shell or pottery. *Orcella* grows more solitarily than *Prunulus*, in light scattered groups, showing an inclination for the neighbourhood of oak trees, and where it does grow it may be found from year to year in the same place, but seldom more than two or three in a spot. In 1869, when *Orcella* was pretty plentiful, *Prunulus* was not to be found in the situations where it usually grows abundantly. *Prunulus* is the reverse of all this. It prefers more shady places, is larger, more fleshy, and with a strong odour, which is rather heavy and overpowering. It grows in greater quantities together, and not unfrequently in crowded rings from four to six feet in diameter. As edible fungi they should certainly be kept distinct. *Orcella* is light and pleasant in odour, and excellent in flavour ; it is so tender and delicate as to be termed, not inaptly, 'vegetable sweetbread.' *Prunulus*, on the other hand, though always good, is to many people too strong in odour, and coarser in taste."

This will dispose of the question of identity as far as our purpose is concerned, and might dispense with any separate reference to them in cooking, save that we are reminded by the same writer quoted above that *Orcella*, being usually found in small quantities, is better when broiled and served on toast. *Prunulus*, growing in greater abundance will serve either for broiling or stewing, or both. *Orcella* should be eaten the same day that it is gathered, either stewed, broiled, or fried with bread and egg crumbs like cutlets. Smith says that, however prepared, it is most excellent, the flesh is firm and juicy, and full of flavour, and whether broiled or stewed, or however prepared, it is a most delicious morsel. In all this we are quite prepared to agree with him, without distinction of *Orcella* or *Prunulus*. Were we to classify edible fungi according to their gastronomic merits, these would find a place in the first class.

XV.—THE CHANTARELLE.

THE most unstinted praise has been lavished on the chantarelle (*Cantharellus cibarius*) from a remote period, and even in our own day, there are some who regard it as unapproachable for excellence. It has one great advantage, that it is attractive in colour and appearance, is by no means uncommon, easily recognized, and cannot well be confounded with any other species, good, bad, or indifferent. Persons without the slightest knowledge of fungi may gather it and eat it with impunity, but it must be cooked carefully and properly, or they may be doomed to disappointment. Battarra, an old writer on fungi, made the remark which has been repeated scores of times, that, if properly prepared, the chantarelle would arrest the pangs of death.

This is a summer fungus, and only a few straggling specimens are to be seen in the great fungus season of September and October, unless the weather is mild. It is found in woods, and not in fields and open pastures; in some parts of the New Forest it is far more plentiful than we have observed it in any other part of England. At times we could have gathered a bushel in an hour or two, but in 1888, 1889, and 1890 all kinds of fungi have been comparatively scarce.

The chantarelle is of a beautiful golden yellow colour in all parts, it is a peculiar yellow, resembling the dark yolk of an egg. In size it is about two inches in breadth and height, and somewhat inversely conical in shape, broadest at the top and gradually decreasing downwards. The top of the cap is flat, and soon depressed, with a thick, lobed, and undulated margin, so that it is always very irregular and often contorted. The flesh of the cap is thick and diminishes gradually into the stem, which in this instance is seldom removed for cooking, as it is of a like texture to the cap. The gills are remarkable, for they are very shallow and thick at the edge, like veins, running down the stem, almost of the same colour as the cap; these veins are also forked, and smaller veins run across transversely from gill to gill. This thick veining, instead of true gill plates, dis-

tinguishes the chantarelle from agarics. The entire
substance of the fungus is dry and opaque, and it has
a peculiar odour, which some have characterised as
that of ripe apricots and others as of plums. When
raw the taste is rather warm. The flesh is whitish,
tinged with the same yellow. It will be seen from
this description that the chantarelle is a unique and
very remarkable fungus.

Berkeley says that "The chantarelle is occasionally
served up at public dinners at the principal hotels in
London, on state occasions, where every effort is
made to secure the rarest and most costly dainties ;"
and Dr Badham writes that "Having collected a
quantity at Tunbridge Wells one summer, and given
them to the cook at the Calverley Hotel to dress, he
learnt from the waiter that they were not novelties to
him ; that, in fact, he had been in the habit of dress-
ing them for years, on state occasions, at the Free-
mason's Tavern." Nevertheless, we confess to never
having seen them exposed for sale in London, although
constantly on the Continent, and never to have recognized them at table, at any dinners, but those memorable ones of the Woolhope Club at Hereford.

The chantarelle is eaten regularly in France, Germany, Austria, and Italy, where it is exposed in the
markets for sale, but it does not seem to be a great
favourite with the poorer classes.

The most approved method of cooking is to pick
and wash the chantarelles, and then allow them to

dry ; they should then be thrown into boiling water, which helps to soften the rather rigid flesh. Afterwards they may be stewed in fresh butter, or olive oil, with chopped tarragon or parsley, pepper, salt, and a little lemon peel : when they are cooked they should be allowed to simmer over a slow fire for fifteen or twenty minutes, and moistened from time to time with beef gravy or cream ; when about to be served the stew is thickened with yolk of egg. Before stewing we prefer them sliced, as this ensures more thorough and uniform cooking.

Another plan, which some will prefer, is simply frying the cut chantarelles in butter or oil, with pepper and salt, adding a few bread crumbs, or pouring them when done over sippets of toast.

The chantarelles may also be cut up small, or minced, and stewed with meat, or gently stewed by themselves, and added to the meat afterwards. Being of a dry nature it must always be remembered that rapid cooking will spoil them by rendering them tough.

If collected in larger quantities than may be required for present use, they may be strung up and dried in the air, but before being used they should always be soaked for a time in water to soften them. They are a useful addition to soups and stews in the winter. In all cases an advantage will be found to accrue from slicing the chantarelles and allowing them to soak all night in milk before stewing or frying them. Weather and locality of growth have also their influences, for in very dry seasons, and when growing in dry spots, the specimens will be small, with an additional tendency to toughness when cooked. No fungus requires more careful preparation than this.

It may be well to refer in this place to a common fungus, which is known as the "false chantarelle," even more common than the true chantarelle, but smaller, of much more slender growth, and not so brightly coloured (*Cantharellus aurantiacus*). It grows amongst grass in open places, and hence rarely to be seen in company with the chantarelle. The cap is seldom more than one and a half inches broad, sometimes one inch, of a pale ochre, but *not* egg yellow, thin and flexible, with gills very close together and numerous, darker than the cap, reddish orange, with a slender pale stem. No one would possibly confound this with the chantarelle after having seen the true species. It has had the reputation of being poisonous, but of this we entertain some doubt, and fancy it is only a tradition : nevertheless, it is not edible, and may cause considerable unpleasantness if eaten. The gills have more the appearance of true gills, rather than veins, on account of their thinness. In some localities a variety is found with very pale, almost white gills, still more unlike the veritable chantarelle. No person with his wits about him could confound the two species, and yet it may be as well to have alluded to it, in order to guard the novice against experimenting with species, which, to him, are doubtful, or unknown. We have for ourselves been addicted to eating a vast number of different kinds of fungi for forty years, and never suffered a moment's inconvenience from the habit, but it must be remembered that we have eaten nothing which we did not know, or which had not a favourable reputation.

XVI.—THE EDIBLE BOLETUS.

HOWEVER delightful it might be theoretically to be able to read a book of this kind without fear of encountering technical names, it is practically impossible to avoid them altogether, except by inventing combinations equally as bad and equally as strange, without the compensation of being accurate. Organisms such as fungi which have excited no interest in the popular mind, have not acquired local names, and as all have been commonly regarded as dangerous and uncanny, no one has taken the trouble to examine them or attempt to discover whether there are any features whereby one kind can be discriminated from another. Yet even the rural school urchin, who is well up in the distinctions between a green-finch and a linnet, or a buttercup and a daisy, could just as readily dis-

criminate between the commoner kinds of the larger
fungi, if there were only vernacular names for them
which could be readily remembered. It would be
worse than useless to invent a host of fancy names,
and associate them in books with the scientific names,
or even with prolix descriptions of the objects themselves, since but few would see or care to read the
books in which the new names are explained. One
remarkable instance of an effort of this kind is present
to our memory, but it only resulted in failure. A
better course to adopt, probably, would be to associate
characteristic names with good coloured portraits of
the objects, but, even in this case, the diffusion of
useful knowledge would be exceedingly limited ; only
a few of the most notable could be selected for
illustration, and some time would elapse before
practical results could be hoped for.

Everyone who has been desirous of extending a
knowledge of fungi has felt this difficulty, and sometimes it has found expression. The writers of books
on this subject, as well as the readers, have been em-
barrassed, and the happy consummation remains as
distant as ever. In this chapter we have to encounter
one of these stumbling blocks, because there is no
real popular designation for the kind of fungi which
botanical people call *Boleti*, as distinguished from
those other fungi which they denominate *Agarics*,
such as the ordinary mushroom represents. It is an
undoubted fact that on the continent of Europe,

where more varied kinds of fungi are extensively eaten than with us, there are a vast number of popular names, but these have probably followed upon the recognition of their alimentary value and not preceded it. The one broad distinction between these two kinds of fungi can be grasped by a very infantile mind, and is not liable to error. The agarics (which include "mushrooms" and "toad-stools" of the vernacular) have plates or gills on the under side of the cap by which they are surmounted, and these plates extend, or radiate from the stem in the centre to the margin of the cap. They may vary exceedingly in number, in colour, in their proximity to each other, and even in thickness, but radiating gills of some kind are always present. In the *Boleti*, on the contrary, there are no gill plates on the under surface of the cap, but their place is occupied by a level surface which is covered with small punctures or perforations, looking as if it had been carefully and regularly pricked with a pin. These pores serve the same purpose in the economy of the plant as the flat surface of the gills in the agarics, but the difference in structure is common to all *Boleti*, in the same manner as gill plates are common to the *Agarics*. We might term these latter "gill-bearing," and the former "pore-bearing" fungi.

If these observations are carefully perused and comprehended, the difference between agarics and boleti will no longer remain a mystery. Cut a

Boletus, such as we have indicated, through the cap
and downwards through the stem, dividing the whole
fungus into two equal halves, and still further light
will be thrown upon its structure. The porous under
surface will usually be different in colour from the
flesh of the cap, and of a considerable thickness, the
pores placed regularly side by side, like small tubes
glued together, and their outer extremity open. The
whole inner surface of these tubes, or pores, produce
the minute seeds, or spores as they should be called,
of the *Boletus*. With this preliminary outline of their
characteristic features, we proceed to note some of
the species which should be sought after for cooking.

We commence with the one which has long been
called the "edible boletus" (*Boletus edulis*) known
and eaten all over the Continent, as well, and as
freely as the "mushroom" is with us. Every little
provision shop in Germany, or Austria, has "ceps"
for sale all the year round. Under this name you
will be supplied with thin slices of *Boletus*, dried in
the air or sun, at a small price per pound, their
general use being an addition to soups or made
dishes. But, to return to the living fungus, which is
common in all parts of the British Isles, during early
autumn, the cap is about the size and colour of a
penny bun ; a nice warm brown quite at the top, and
paler towards the edge. The most common diameter
will be three to four inches, but it is not unusual for
them to reach as much as seven or eight inches

across, with a corresponding increase in thickness.
The pore surface is a light greenish yellow, paler
when young, sunk to a channel round the stem. It
often happens that the stem is much deformed,
always thick and solid, not less than an inch thick
at the top, and twice as thick at the base, commonly
five or six inches in length. In colour it approaches
a warm ochre, and the upper part of the stem is
covered with a minute reticulation or network of fine
veins, which are but little darker than the ground
colour of the stem, and sometimes so nearly of the
same colour as to be scarcely distinguishable. There
is a little clamminess about the top of the cap in wet
weather, but this is not perceptible when the weather
is fine and dry. There is no distinctive odour, and
the taste of the flesh, especially when young, is sweet
and nutty. When cut through, or broken, the flesh
does *not* immediately, or at any time, become of a
deep blue. It will be borne in mind that all the
Boleti which change colour to a deep blue when cut
or bruised are not only suspicious, but some are
strongly poisonous. The same remark may be
made of *Boleti* as of other fungi, that young specimens are sweeter and more tender than when fully
matured, and that they cannot be too fresh when
eaten. "High game" is not applicable to fungi.
The edible boletus grows mostly in woods, and is not
readily confounded with any other species; certainly
not when it has once been satisfactorily determined.

In whatever way it is prepared for the table it is preferable to discard the stems, and cut away the porous portion which occupies the under surface of the cap. This reduces the bulk to carry home, and, when found, it is usually in company, and there is no need to fear a short supply at the proper season. Some persons take objection to this fungus as food, on the ground that it is rather mucilaginous. We venture to think that it is not sufficiently so to depreciate it in general estimation, provided the porous portion is excluded. Sliced and dried it may be preserved through the winter to form an ingredient in soups and stews.

Dried boleti are made into soup in some parts of Europe. The dried "ceps" are soaked in warm water until they become softened ; they are then stewed with the usual condiments, and thickened with toasted bread. It is quite permissible to add gravy, or any other seasonable adjunct.

The simplest method consists in removing the stem and pores, and cutting up the fleshy cap into small pieces, which are laid in a dish with butter, pepper, and salt, covered close, and baked for an hour.

A more elaborate method is given by Persoon, who says that they may be cooked with white sauce, with or without chicken, in fricassee, broiled or baked with butter, salad oil, pepper, salt, chopped herbs, and bread crumbs ; to which some add ham, or a little anchovy. They make excellent fritters.

Some roast them with onions (basting with butter), but as the onions take longer to cook than the boletus, the latter must not be added until the former have begun to soften.

Dr Badham says that the best method of cooking this fungus must be left to the taste of the individual interested. In every way it is good. "Its tender and juicy flesh, its delicate and sapid flavour, render it equally acceptable to the plain and to the accomplished cook. It imparts a relish alike to the homely hash and the dainty ragoût, and may be truly said to improve every dish of which it is a constituent." Whilst the Rev. M. J. Berkeley wrote that "Though much neglected in this country, it appears to be a most valuable article of food. It resembles much in taste the common mushroom, and is quite as delicate : it abounds in seasons when these are not to be found."

A novel method of cooking this fungus has been recommended by Mr Edwin Lees, but we have never tested it. He says," It should not be disguised with any sauce beyond lemon juice and powdered lump sugar ; in fact, as part of a fungus dinner it should come last with the puddings and sweets. As a fricassee or sweet omelette it is excellent, and when thus delicately cooked has a close resemblance to custard pudding." Another plan of preparation is thus described— Remove the stems and pores from the fungi, and divide the remainder into half inch slices. Take six

H

or eight ounces of lean uncooked ham, cut into small squares, and put them in a large stewpan, adding a large wineglass of the best salad oil, and fry for a few minutes, until the ham takes a pale yellowish colour ; then add the pieces of boletus, and fry for another five minutes ; remove from the fire, and add a tea-spoonful of common salt, a salt spoonful of crushed (not ground) black pepper, one large sweet Spanish red pepper cut in pieces (but if not to be procured substitute a fresh green chili) a little nutmeg, and a teaspoonful of chopped parsley ; add a large wineglass-ful of sherry. Then place it on the fire, the lid of the stewpan closely shut down, and let it stew gently for three quarters of an hour ; stir in the juice of half a lemon, and serve up hot.

XVII.—OTHER BOLETI.

JUST at the time of year when the edible boletus is going off, and becoming scarce, another species nearly as large, and some think equally good, is making its appearance. Of course the two are often found together, but the plentiful season for one is in advance of that of the other. As soon as the supply of the " edible " slackens, the "rough legged " (*Boletus scaber*) comes in to take its place. This boletus, which is so common in woods in October, is not quite so broad in the cap as the other. It reaches from three to seven inches in diameter, but is most usual about four inches. The cap is very convex, almost hemispherical at first, but in expanding becoming less so, viscid and smooth, usually dull brown, but also greyish, and a common form is brick red, or terra cotta. Sometimes the cap is minutely downy, with the down collected in little tufts, but often so slightly velvety as not to be observable without a pocket lens. The flesh is very thick and white in young specimens, but usually turning reddish grey when cut or broken, if fully mature. The tubes are very long, becoming short next the stem, and the under surface is of a dirty white, often smoky. There is a deep channel round the top of the stem, caused by the shortening of the tubes. The stem is six inches long, thicker at the base and attenuated gradually upwards, dirty white, and rough throughout its length, with blackish dot like scales, sometimes arranged in lines. This roughness of the stem is peculiarly characteristic. It will be observed that the stem is invariably thinner above than in the edible boletus and more attenuated. It is not unusual for the stem to be much thickened and distorted at the base, but always more or less rough. There is no species with which it can be confounded, unless it be one which in this country we call *versipellis*, and that is equally good-eating, and may, after all, be nothing more than a variety. The flesh is firmer and less mucilaginous than the edible boletus, hence it is preferred by some people.

There is a larger, but, unfortunately, rare species which is earlier in appearance than either of those we have described.   The summer boletus (*Boletus æstivalis*) reaches sometimes a diameter of ten inches, and the cap varies from pale tan colour to grey; it is silky, and often covered with a frosty bloom.   As it becomes old the surface cracks into angular or irregular patches.   The under surface is whitish, and the thick flesh does not change colour when cut. Special caution should be taken not to attempt cooking any species the flesh of which changes to blue when cut.   Some of the worst species become of a deep indigo blue immediately on being cut or broken.   The stem in this species is two inches thick, moderately long, and a little tapering upwards, of a dull whitish colour, and even.   It is mostly found in pastures, under trees, sometimes as early as May, but most commonly in June or July.   Mrs Hussey says that this is the most delicious of all the boleti, and Dr Bull was of the same opinion.   Perhaps one of the reasons why it has not been found more often is the early period of its appearance, before fungus eaters as a rule think of going out in search of spoil.

There is a species which is found occasionally on woodsides later in the year, which has the reputation of being esculent (*Boletus impolitus*).   It often attains a large size, and resembles the above in form, and in some other features, but the under surface of the cap is yellowish, and the flesh turns faintly blue when cut. It is this latter feature which precludes our recommending it, as it is better to have no exception to the rule of discarding all species which turn blue when cut. This is one of the rarer species, and therefore would be no material accession to our list of edible species. In view of the possibility of error, it is better to remain on the safe side.

Amongst small species the one which has given us the greatest satisfaction has been the "granular boletus" (*Boletus granulatus*). It has been seldom recommended, and yet we prefer it to the edible boletus, or indeed any other that we have tried. It is one of the group which has a glutinous, sticky cap, and grows on the ground under fir trees. The colour is that peculiar warm, pinkish yellow, almost indescribable, which some call gilvous, and which we have likened to the surface of a sponge cake. A great number of specimens will always be found growing together, and the cap is seldom much over two inches broad, at first convex, and then flattened with a little convexity ; it is covered with a thick slime, which makes the cap appear of a darker colour, until it disappears, leaving only a little stickiness behind. The flesh is white, with a slight yellowish tinge, and rather firm. The pores on the under surface are whitish at first, and then lemon coloured, with the edges moist and granular, as if powdered with sugar.

The stem is one or two inches long, and about half an inch thick, yellowish, the upper part granulated with little points, without a collar or ring, but often sprinkled with little drops as if of exuded moisture. The tubes should be removed before cooking.

A bright yellow species (*Boletus elegans*), also found under fir trees, is reputed to be good eating. The cap is convex, golden yellow, very viscid, from two to three inches in diameter, the under surface is of a sulphury yellow, and the mouth of the pores angular, running a little way down the stem. The stem is usually cylindrical, almost equal, four inches long, and half an inch thick, pale yellow at first, then reddish, with a pendulous collar or ring in the upper portion, above the ring punctate with little dots. The flesh is of a pale yellow, and rather firm. Although this species is common enough, we have never tried its edible qualities, having been sufficiently satisfied with the granular boletus.

Some of our friends have commended the "bay boletus" (*Boletus badius*), although we have always suspected it to be only second rate. It delights most in pine woods, and the cap is convex, which it maintains, about three or four inches in diameter, soft and sticky in wet weather, but rather shining when dry, of a tawny bay colour, darker when wet and then deep bay ; pores rather large and angular, of a dingy yellowish white at first, and at length greenish. The stem is nearly equal throughout, erect, and four or more inches long, three quarters of an inch thick, paler than the cap, apparently frosted with brown. When cut the flesh is dirty white, but it has a tendency here and there to become blue. For this reason, if for no other, we repeat the caution to beginners not to eat this or any other species which turns blue, unless it has been identified and recommended by some competent person. For ourselves we should not hesitate to eat the " bay boletus," but then we should first satisfy ourselves that it was *that* species, and no other, previous to the experiment.

Boleti are certainly fond of growing under fir trees, for there is another rather common species found in such situations, which, if not enticing in appearance, has been commended. The dingy boletus (*Boletus bovinus*), or as the latin name implies, "oxen" boletus grows in companies, with a cap about two inches broad, smooth and viscid, almost slimy, reddish grey, dull yellow, or deep buff, paler at the margin, which is whitish and woolly, stem two or three inches high, and one half to three quarters of an inch thick, of the same colour as the cap, sometimes attenuated below, and streaked with watery lines. Flesh tinged with the general colour, but unchangeable. Pores angular, very shallow, and compound, dirty yellow, becoming rusty when old. It has a strong odour resembling that of the fairy-ring champignon. As an edible species it has been compared with the granular boletus.

The chestnut boletus (*Boletus castaneus*) is distinguished from all the other species we have named by its white, afterwards yellowish spores. It is not common in woods, but is a neat, clean-looking species. The cap is about three inches in diameter, depressed when old, and then shallow concave, of a dark rufous tan colour and velvety; the flesh is thick, coloured beneath the cuticle like the cap, but not changing colour, the stem is variable in length, and almost equal, of a cinnamon colour, without a ring. The pores on the under side of the cap are white, then dirty yellow, free from the stem. There are but scanty references to this as an edible species, and we have not met with any one but ourselves in this country who has cooked and eaten it. Still we give the preference to *Boletus granulatus*.

There are other kinds which have been suggested or recommended, but we have given sufficient, and those omitted are not equal to those inserted. Mr Worthington Smith writes—" Before I properly knew *Boletus edulis*, I ate all sorts of boleti in mistake for it, notably *Boletus chrysenteron*." This latter species we should not have included under any circumstances, since some report it as suspicious, and others as " nasty."

XVIII.—VEGETABLE BEEF STEAK.

THE only successful manner of justifying this rather extraordinary title would be a practical demonstration, which we must leave our readers to do for themselves, if we can only induce them to make the experiment. It is not a name of our own, but one which is tolerably familiar to fungus eaters. Another is "ox tongue," or oak tongue, or tongue of chestnut, from its resemblance, when young, both in form and colour to a tongue. In this country it is usually found on old oaks, but in Italy it is found also on the chestnut. The popular names by which this fungus is known on the Continent stand in evidence that it is recognised by the people generally as something in which they have an interest, that it is a popular object, for only popular objects get for themselves popular names. In spite of our insular prejudices, even the "vegetable beef steak" is gradually becoming known, and persons with no general knowledge of fungi have learnt to know and appreciate this comparatively new article of food. There is quite sufficient individuality about this fungus for it to become well known, and readily recognised, without the most rudimentary knowledge of fungi, as readily as a beetroot is known without a knowledge of botany.

The first appearance of growth is a small reddish knob on the tree upon which it is to flourish, like a strawberry, and this gradually grows and enlarges until it becomes like an ox tongue, or part of a bullock's liver. It projects from the tree to which it is attached, without a stem, and although variable in shape is often semicircular, six, eight, or ten inches across, and two or three inches thick behind, gradu ally thinner towards the margin. The upper surface is liver coloured, at first rather rough but soon be- coming smooth, the under surface is flesh coloured, growing darker with age. If the under surface is carefully examined, it will seem to be punctured all over with little pinholes, and these are the mouths of the tubes, which are closely packed, side by side, like the tubes of a boletus, only that they separate from each other readily. If cut in any direction the flesh presents a mottled appearance somewhat like beet- root, and as juicy. The whole upper surface exudes a kind of sticky moisture, so that it is rather clammy to the touch. The odour which it possesses is sug- gestive of wine, and its taste distinctly acid but not unpleasant. Specimens vary considerably in size, but one of two or three pounds weight is not un- common. Dr Badham records that he once found one which measured nearly five feet round, and weighed upwards of eight pounds, whilst the Rev. M. J. Berkeley is the authority for one which weighed nearly thirty pounds.

In the case of agarics it is understood that young specimens, or at least before fully matured, are the most delicate and best for the table. This order is reversed with the beef steak fungus, which is best when it is fully ripe or matured. The young fungus, growing upon oak, appears to obtain too much tannin from the tree, so that it is bitter or astringent, and by no means attractive, but when quite mature all astringency has vanished, and the fungus is in its prime. So long as decay has not commenced this sort of beef steak, like game, should be rather high. It is an excellent provision for the benefit of fungus eaters of every degree, that it is very rare to find a vegetable beef steak maggotty. We have gathered specimens too numerous to mention, and cannot remember a single instance in which they were so attacked. Lovers of *Fistulina hepatica* are recommended always to note, and note down, a tree whereon it is found, because the probabilities are strongly in favour of its occurring annually on that same tree, and in the same spot, for many consecutive years. This is not supposition but the result of many a fortunate experience.

The *Fistulina* is an excellent illustration of the mistake so common to most persons who have little experience of fungus eating. That mistake consists in taking the common mushroom as the type, and supposing that all others must resemble it in such manner as to be a substitute for it, or replace it.

There is present no other idea but that of the peculiar mushroom flavour, of the heavy mushroom odour. All other species are approached with this preconceived notion, are tested by this arbitrary test, and failure is a result easily predicated. Against this assumption too strong a protest cannot well be made. No one presumes that all animal food is precisely the same; that beef and mutton and venison and fowl are different names for the same thing. Each has its own individual flavour, and no one seeks to compare them with any other which may be arbitrarily set up as the type of animal food. It is the same with the edible fungi to a large extent, since each kind has its own peculiarity and is the better for a peculiar mode of treatment. It is simply courting disappointment to anticipate that all are alike, except in form and name, whilst in fact no two kinds are so absolutely alike as to be indistinguishable by an educated palate. Hence, then, it would follow that the methods of preparation for the table may be supposed to differ, and that a method which is the most successful with one kind will not be the best for another. These are details which experience will soon impress upon us, and there is no more fitting example for the test than the subject of the present chapter.

Subject to this reservation, that it is an esculent to be judged solely on its own merits, we find Mrs Hussey writing of it that " If it is not beef itself it is the sauce for it," and the dictum of the Rev. M. J. Berkeley that it was "One of the best things he ever ate, but then it was prepared by a skilful cook." Or, again, Mr Worthington Smith, who writes, "It is truly a vegetable beef steak, for the taste resembles meat in a remarkable manner. It is good broiled with a steak and properly seasoned. There is a slight but very perceptible acid flavour with it, which gives considerable zest and piquancy to the dish, rendering it a treat for an epicure."

In France it is first washed and dried then placed in boiling water for a short time, and afterwards stewed with butter, parsley, scallion, pepper, and salt, yolk of egg being afterwards added when the stew is ready for the table. In Vienna it is sliced in thin slices, and eaten in salad as we eat beetroot.

Its chief use and value is in furnishing a kind of sauce or gravy, and for this Mrs Hussey has supplied a method. Slice and macerate the fungus with salt, after the manner of making mushroom ketchup. The deep, red liquor that is produced should be put into a dish with a little lemon juice, and minced shallots, and a broiled rump steak deposited in it. This liquor is not catsup for it has but little of the flavour of mushroom, but it is a beef gravy of high virtue.

Dr Badham says that the best way to dress it, if old, is to stew it down for stock, and reject the flesh ; if young, it may be eaten in substance, plain or with minced meat ; in all cases its succulency is such that it furnishes its own sauce.

An ordinary and expeditious method is to slice up the *Fistulina* and fry it together with rump steak, to which it furnishes a savoury addition. Of course it may be fried and eaten by itself, but it gives more satisfaction when simply treated as a sauce.

XIX.—PUFF BALLS.

OUR earliest acquaintance with the great puff ball (*Lycoperdon giganteum*) was made in the country, amongst the cottagers of an agricultural population. Old and dried specimens, entire, or in parts, were carefully preserved for use, in one of two ways, but neither of them gastronomic. In those days it was considered that a fragment of the woolly interior mass, with its profusion of minute snuff-coloured spores, was the best of all remedies to apply for the staunching of blood in wounds. Elderly dames, who in small villages acquire a reputation in the healing art, preserved fragments year after year, for use in cases of emergency, and the readiest and most common application for a deep cut was to bind a piece of " puff ball " over the wound, and allow it to remain until healed. The other use was for stupefy-ing bees when the natives had a design upon their honey. These, and no other, were believed to be the reasons why puff balls were sent into the world, excepting, perhaps, certain schoolboys who imagined that Providence had supplied them to their hands as instruments of torture to be applied to their fellows, by an outward application to noses and eyes.

The danger of the latter mode of utilizing the puff ball was illustrated at Edinburgh a few years since. The assistant to a learned professor, making preparation for a coming lecture, was industriously operating upon a large puff ball, which had been kept exposed and covered with dust. In order to remove this dust and make the specimen fit for exhibition on the lecture table, it was brushed and beaten so that a perfect cloud of the minute spores enveloped the unsuspecting operator. These minute bodies found entrance by his mouth and nostrils, with such effect that he was confined to his bed for many days, under the care of most competent medical men, and narrowly escaped with his life.

In Norfolk these large puff balls, found at the margins of corn fields in harvest time, are locally known as "Bulfers," or, as some prefer to write it, "Bullfists," and in other counties they appear also to have local names, so that they are well known to the natives. In all stages they have a sinister reputation, and we remember the horror caused on one occasion by our determination to have a portion of one cooked for our own consumption. On all hands it was declared to be "rank pi'sen," and no one would undertake to help us "shuffle off this mortal coil." This may be the reason why men and boys persist in knocking and kicking them to atoms whenever found.

There is a tradition of olden time, in the days of " flint and steel," that housewives employed the dried substance of this fungus as tinder, and old Gerarde remarks that " In divers parts of England, where people doth dwell farre from neighbours, they carry them kindled with fire, which lasteth long." In allusion to some of the old customs, it is written—

> " The aged Puff balls shall help us to cheat
> The dainty bees of their luscious meat ;
> While others shall turn to give us light,
> And scare from our dell the dreary night."

The giant puff ball is sometimes not larger than a moderately sized turnip, but it is not uncommonly " as big as a man's head." We have met with them a foot in diameter, but never so large as a recumbent sheep, as narrated of one in America.

Professor Bessey says it was of an oval outline, and measured five feet four in its longest diameter, and four feet six inches in its smallest diameter, whilst its height was but nine and a half inches. Professor Call says of it that it was much larger than the largest washtub we have at home. Only imagine a slice from such a puff ball fried for breakfast—only a

yard and a half long. A fairly good-sized specimen was recorded in the *Gardener's Chronicle* (September 20, 1884), which was five feet four inches in circumference, but that would give only a diameter of about twenty-one inches, with which we must "rest and be thankful."

The form of the giant puff ball is oval, sometimes nearly globose, depressed a little at the top, and of a pure white colour, without and within, so long as it remains fit for food. The surface is smooth and soft like kid leather, but at length cracking. As it ripens it becomes discoloured and dry. The interior is at first, and for a long time, pure white, juicy but firm, so as to be cut easily like a turnip. Afterwards it turns sulphury yellow, and finally olive, when it is resolved into a mass of delicate threads mixed with a profusion of minute spores, like snuff. It is only in the immature condition, and whilst the interior remains fleshy and perfectly white, that it is edible.

It grows on the borders of fields, in orchards, sometimes in meadows, and occasionally in gardens, being juicy and good about the end of July or August, reaching the powdery state in September. In agricultural districts it is always sought for in harvest time, if intended to be eaten. Usually it is found singly, or only two or three together, but occasionally they form a segment of a large ring. Unfortunately the mystery of cultivation has not been solved.

I

A few years since a friend occupied a house on Wandsworth Common, and adjoining was an enclosed ground plot intended to be built upon. By arrangement with the landlord the use of this plot was secured to our friend as a rough kitchen garden and playground for his children. On a visit we remarked a preserved portion of some two or three square yards, protected by thorns, &c. Upon enquiry it was ascertained that large puff balls had come up on this spot, and of course had been appropriated and eaten. The protection had been supplied in hopes of a crop in the succeeding year, if the ground was not trodden or disturbed. These hopes were realized, for on the following, and succeeding years, the puff balls came up on the same spot, until the builders appropriated the plot, and a villa was reared where the puff balls used to grow. For many years our friend had a succession of puff balls for the table, and duly appreciated the privilege.

It is a curious experience in connection with this fungus that although we have introduced and recommended it as food to a large number of persons, we have never discovered one who did not approve of it. One incident we have related before will bear repetition. "A gardener brought us a large puff ball, equal in size to a half quartern loaf, which was still in its young and pulpy state, of a beautiful creamy whiteness when cut. It had been found developing itself in a garden at Highgate, and to the finder its virtues were unknown. We had this specimen cut in slices of about half an inch in thickness, or rather less, the outer skin peeled off, and each slice dipped in egg which had been beaten up, then sprinkled with bread crumbs, and fried in butter, with salt and pepper. The result was exceedingly satisfactory; and finding this immense fungus more than our family could consume whilst it remained fresh, we invited several friends to partake, and they were as delighted as ourselves with the new relish; some at first declined, but gradually one after another fell in, until the whole united in a first, but certainly not the last, experiment upon fried puff ball."

The testimony of the late Rev. Dr Curtis proves that the giant puff ball is duly appreciated in the United States, for he writes—"It is a great favourite with me as it is indeed with all my acquaintances who have tried it. It has not the high aroma of some others, but it has a delicacy of flavour that makes it superior to any omelette I have ever eaten. It seems furthermore to be so digestible as to adapt itself to the most delicate stomachs. It is the South Down of mushrooms."

The instructions for cooking are in all cases limited to a few words, and the suggested processes are all very similar. One says—Cut in slices half an inch thick, it may be simply broiled or fried with butter, pepper, and salt, and when served up hot will meet with general approbation. Another says—Cut slices half an inch thick, dip in yolk of egg, sprinkle with pepper, salt, and sweet herbs, fry in fresh butter, and serve hot. Another says—Fry the half inch slices in fresh butter, with a very slight sprinkling of salt, and any preserve that might be available, and serve hot. Our own method has been to cut the slices less than half an inch thick, cover them with egg beaten up, and sprinkle with bread crumbs, fry them until the surface is browned, like a fried sole, and then serve. Of course pepper and salt are better sprinkled over before frying. The universality with which this dish is appreciated is more remarkable than with any other fungus which we have introduced to our friends. We have no recollection of a single instance in which it was not approved.

There are several kinds of smaller puff balls which are common on lawns, heaths, and pastures ; these are doubtless harmless in the young state, and whilst the flesh is pure white. They have been recommended as food, cooked in the same way as the giant puff ball, but we have never tried them, chiefly on account of their small size. On no account should any puff ball be cooked after the flesh has commenced discolouration.

XX.—BUFF CAPS AND IVORY CAPS.

MOST persons who have taken sufficient interest in growing fungi to notice them will be familiar with the form and colour of a peculiar buff tinted mushroom, which comes up on lawns and pastures in the autumn. Several will have been seen growing together amongst the grass, so that occasionally a good basketful may be collected in ten minutes. We have called this the "buff caps" (*Hygrophorus pratensis*) for lack of a better name. And yet the colour is hardly "buff," and hardly fawn colour, and not flesh colour, but something of a combination of all, which goes by the name of gilvous. The mushroom in question is a clean, neat-growing species, with a cap two or three inches broad, smooth and soft, like a tan coloured kid glove, and at first very convex, but afterwards more flattened. When cut through it will be observed that the flesh is very thick, especially at the centre of the cap, tapering downwards into the stem, which is rather short, and a little lighter in colour than the cap, and thinnest at the base. The gills are distant from each other, so that the cross veins can be seen which run between them, comparatively broad, running some distance down the stem, so that they are arched, until when old the

cap is flattened, the colour being the same as that of
the cap. It has rather a pleasant, but not very
decided odour, and mild taste. The colour is not a
common one even amongst fungi, and there is but
little chance of confounding it with any other ; but it
should be remembered that it does not grow in
woods, but in open places, on lawns, and especially
downs, amongst short grass, that the gills are wide
apart, and run a long way down the stem, and no
mistake is possible. Opinions may be divided as to
whether this should be considered as a mushroom of
the first class, as an esculent, or only second rate,
which depends much on cooking ; at all events it is
thoroughly wholesome, and of a delicate flavour.

"Ivory caps" (*Hygrophorus virgineus*) is of a
smaller size than "buff caps," and grows in damper
places, to a very late period of the season, regardless
of frost, unless it is very sharp and sudden. It is
wholly white as snow, and though small is conspicuous amongst the green grass. The cap is one or two
inches broad, soon expanded and flattened, viscid
when moist, and even slimy in very wet weather.
The stem is short, and the gills are continued from
the edge of the cap down the stem, so as to form an
inverted cone. They are distant apart and broad, so
that the veins at the base may be distinctly seen
passing from gill to gill. No appreciable odour can
be distinguished, and the taste is mild. The only other
pure white species found amongst grass is also edible,

so that there is nothing with which it could be confounded.

There is a rather larger species in woods, with a longer stem (*Hygrophorus eburneus*) which is also edible. It is pure white, and rather slimy, the cap is convex, two or three inches broad, and shining when dry. The stem is twice as long as the diameter of the cap, with the upper part sprinkled with minute point like scales, the gills reach the stem but are not continued down it. The specimens are scattered, but by no means uncommon. We could never detect any odour, although there is a similar species, with a brownish tint in the centre of the cap, which possesses a strong, unpleasant odour like that of the larvæ of the goat moth. As far as their esculent properties are concerned we do not recognise any difference between the woodland and the pasture species. The strong smelling species we have never been tempted to eat; it probably is quite harmless, but has no reputation as an esculent species, still we have no fondness for original research where the stomach is the test.

The *Hygrophori* have hitherto hardly received the justice which is due to them as articles of food. One advantage they certainly possess which should not be overlooked, and that is their general innocence of harm. We cannot indicate a single species which is positively known to be poisonous, although suspicions have always hovered about two species common amongst grass late in the season—the one with a conical green and yellow cap, and the other with a conical yellowish cap soon turning black when bruised or old. However, we are concerned now with two species which are common and *not* unclean. The pasture hygrophorus (*H. pratensis*) is universally recognised as "perfectly wholesome," but as it is a somewhat dry fungus requires care in cooking to prevent its being condemned as tough. Dr Bull wrote of it that it was " A very excellent fungus, of pleasant appearance, agreeable odour, and delicate flavour."

The ivory caps (*Hygrophorus virgineus*) and its smaller white companion (*H. niveus*) are worthy of more attention than fungus eaters have given to them. This may be predicated from the fact that no special modes of cooking have been recommended for them beyond "stew gently with fine herbs and delicate sauce." Both require the addition of gravy, and as the Woolhope record intimates—"They should be stewed very gently for an hour, with the usual condiments, closely covered up, and served hot." Like all mushrooms of dry texture that require cooking for some time to make them tender, it is necessary to keep the temperature low, that the delicate flavour may not be lost. The white species are not so dry as the pasture hygrophorus, and the late Dr Chapman has remarked that they have the flavour of the fairy ring champignon, but are more tender and delicate, and either boiled or fried are an excellent dish for the breakfast table.

There is, however, another *Hygrophorus* which cannot be omitted, since it is one of the most splendid in colour and delicate in flavour. This is the large crimson species found on lawns in the latter days of autumn (*Hygrophorus coccineus*). There is no fungus with which it can be confounded save one, and that is another species of the same genus, which is also edible, and hence there is no danger. The cap is obtusely conical, two inches in height, or more, of a bright crimson, but soon turning pale at the top ; in expanding it usually splits in the line of the gills, for the substance of the cap is rather thin ; it is elevated upon a hollow reddish stem, an inch longer than the cap, and the gills are tinged with crimson. It is a most unmistakable object, and has been depicted in books and pictures over and over again. Until recently we did not attempt to verify the report that it was excellent eating, but having found some half a dozen tempting specimens, we made drawings of them first and devoured them afterwards. Grilled with a piece of butter, salt and pepper, and served on toast they proved to be most delicate and delicious. There was not the slightest indication of toughness, for indeed the entire fungus is so tender and fragile that such a condition was never feared ; but we were scarcely prepared to experience such a delicacy as it proved to be.

XXI.—THE OYSTER MUSHROOM.

THERE is a general impression amongst novices in the art of fungus eating that none of the species which are found growing upon trees are good food, and many of them positively deleterious. This, however, is too sweeping a condemnation which is not borne out by fact. It is true that the most delicious of edible fungi do not grow upon trees, but upon the ground; still there are several species which grow habitually upon decayed wood that are not only innocuous, but also very good for food. Some of these it shall be our endeavour to describe as clearly as we can, commencing with one of the largest, although, perhaps, not quite the best.

The oyster mushroom (*Agaricus ostreatus*) is a very common fungus on fallen trees, stumps, and standing trees which have commenced decay. It is a tufted, or cœspitose species, growing in dense overlapping clusters of twenty or thirty individuals, so that the cluster is very often a foot in diameter. The stems are lateral, short, and rather thick, and the gills are white. The spores also are white, and may often be seen lying like hoar frost on any object which may lie beneath the gills. The whole fungus is moist and fleshy, soft to the touch, especially in damp weather, but not viscid. It is essential, however, that we describe the whole fungus in detail, as intelligibly as we can, without resorting to technicalities.

The caps are closely imbricated, or overlapping, like the tiles of a house. Each individual pileus is somewhat fan shaped, or forming three parts of a circle, some are two or three, and others five or six inches in diameter. The central portion, and backwards, is rather depressed. The whole colour is usually ashy grey, becoming tawny, and at length paler with age, or in dry weather. The flesh of the cap is thick and white, with a pleasant taste. The edge of the cap is at first turned in, and delicately downy, soon becoming smooth. The margin is almost always palest, and often cracks as it expands. The whole surface is smooth and shining when dry. The stem is short and curved ; the gills are quite white and broad, running down the stem, where they become very narrow, ultimately like veins, with cross veins between them, almost like a raised network on the stem. The whole fungus has a strong mushroomy odour, but not unpleasant.

There is a variety of this fungus which has the caps of a bluish grey, with the centre turning of a tawny brown with age. Some have considered it a distinct species, and called it *columbinus* from its dove-colour, but for our purpose it may be regarded as a variety, as it is equally good to eat. Certain enthusiasts have imagined that this species has somewhat the flavour of oysters, although we fear they have been carried away by their imagination. Having had some experience in the flavour of oysters, and also in that of the oyster mushroom, we regret to confess that our imagination did not suggest a resemblance. It is a firm, fleshy fungus, and when slowly and carefully cooked, a pleasant and digestible one, but it may be spoiled by bad treatment, and any way, we prefer the elm tree mushroom, hereafter described.

The methods of cooking for all the species included in this chapter would be identical, and hence may be relegated to the end.

Some misapprehension has filled the minds of persons who should have known better, that another species, very similar to the above in all essential particulars, is unsafe and possibly deleterious. Having eaten it ourselves we can at once dispel the illusion, and affirm that the *Agaricus euosmus* is quite as good, and equally trustworthy, with the oyster mushroom. As already indicated, the two are almost identical in appearance and colour, so that the description of one will apply generally to the other, with this one exception, that in *Agaricus euosmus* there is a faint pinkish tinge about the gills, and the spores as they fall are *not* of a pure white but of a very pale rose colour, with a slight suggestion of violet, and the odour is a little different, possessing a resemblance to tarragon. It is not so common as the oyster mushroom, and usually makes its appearance earlier in the year, at the end of spring, or commencement of summer, although it even extends into August.

It is only during the past three or four years that another edible fungus has been recognised as growing on elm trees in this country, and yet now it has been seen in half a dozen places remote from each other. This (*Agaricus sapidus*) is smaller than the foregoing, and the clusters are not so large or dense, seldom more than half a dozen growing together; the stems are confluent, or grown into each other, so as to form a sort of common branched stem. The caps are orbicular, about two or three inches across, and deeply depressed in the centre; they do not overlap as in the other species, and hence present a different appearance when growing. In colour it is usually white, but occasionally with tints of brown. The flesh is always white, and sweet to the taste. There is little or no perceptible odour. As an esculent it scarcely differs from the oyster mushroom, or, if anything, it is a little more delicate. There is something very tantalising about this species, in that it will be seen growing high up a standing elm, for it grows mostly on standing timber, on a dead branch, or at the side of a hollow in the trunk, some twenty or thirty feet from the ground.

We must not omit the genuine elm mushroom, one of our oldest favourites (*Agaricus ulmarius*), and, if our opinion goes for anything, the best of all this

group of tree agarics. It is so common that it may
be seen growing in September on almost every decaying elm (and decaying elms are by no means
rare); often again, unfortunately, high up in the
tree. We have a vivid recollection of an excursion
during which one of the party ventured to climb an
old elm to secure a splendid specimen of this fungus,
which was many inches across, and a white nutty
flesh, more than an inch in thickness. The fungus
came down, and so did the climber, for he trusted to
a rotten bough, and both descended together. Poor
fellow, his excursion was ended for that day, and it
was some time before he recovered wholly, although
no bones were broken. The fungus was so large
that it was divided between three or four persons,
each of whom had a good meal, for it was in a prime
condition.

This reminds us that we have not yet attempted to
describe the elm tree mushroom. It does not grow
in clusters, or not more than three or four together in
a clump, sometimes only one, but it attains a large
size, six to nine inches in diameter, with a thick,
white flesh. The colour of the cap is a creamy
white, turning a little rusty in the centre when old.
It is almost round, or rather elongated, and fan
shaped with a thick, curved, oblique stem, entering
the cap away from the centre, towards one side, so
that it is what is termed *excentric*. Upwards it is
smooth, but rather woolly below, expanding into the

cap. The gills are very broad, according to the size of the cap. In the large specimen named above they were nearly an inch, and comparatively thick, broadest in the centre; attenuated towards the margin and abrupt behind, with a notch, or rounded, but not running down the stem as in all the species mentioned above. The gills are of a creamy yellow, so that when cut through in section, they contrast against the pure white flesh. It has a very pleasant taste when raw, and can be eaten with sandwiches on a foray day with much satisfaction. There is so little tendency to decay that it will remain perfectly good and edible for several days.

There are two or three others of the same group of tree agarics with a one-sided stem which are re-commended as edible, but these are mostly too rare in this country to warrant their insertion here, inasmuch as a fungus which has to be hunted for diligently, and not found more than once in ten years, can hardly be relied upon as an article of food.

It may not be out of place here to call attention to the fact that we do not suspect any one of our indigenous species of agaric, such as we have described, with *white* spores, and a one-sided stem, to be other than thoroughly harmless. We might as well add that we believe them all to be wholesome, even though some might be rather tough. This assurance may give courage to those who feel nervous, under

an old prejudice, that fungi found growing on trees
are not fit for food.

The methods of cooking hitherto adopted for these
fungi are by no means elaborate.   It is always
advisable to discard the stems in all the fungi of
this type, that is, all of the agaric or mushroom
kind, because they are of a tougher substance, and at
the best would be indigestible.   Unless the surface
of the cap is warty or scaly, it is unnecessary to
attempt to remove the cuticle or skin, which is not
often easily separable.   It is quite eligible to slice
any of these fungi, or cut them into equal sized
pieces, and after the addition of salt and pepper to
stew them, adding sweet herbs, and thickening with
flour when nearly ready, stewing gently until uniformly soft.   Of course gravy may be added, or
meat or fowl according to each individual conscience.

We have proved that the elm fungus may be cut
in slices, sprinkled with pepper and salt, and fried,
with or without bacon, but if without, then with
butter, gravy, or stock, or some other moisture to
prevent burning.   In like manner the slices may be
placed in a stew pan with the usual condiments, and
an addition of sweet herbs, or a few slices of onion
when not disagreeable.

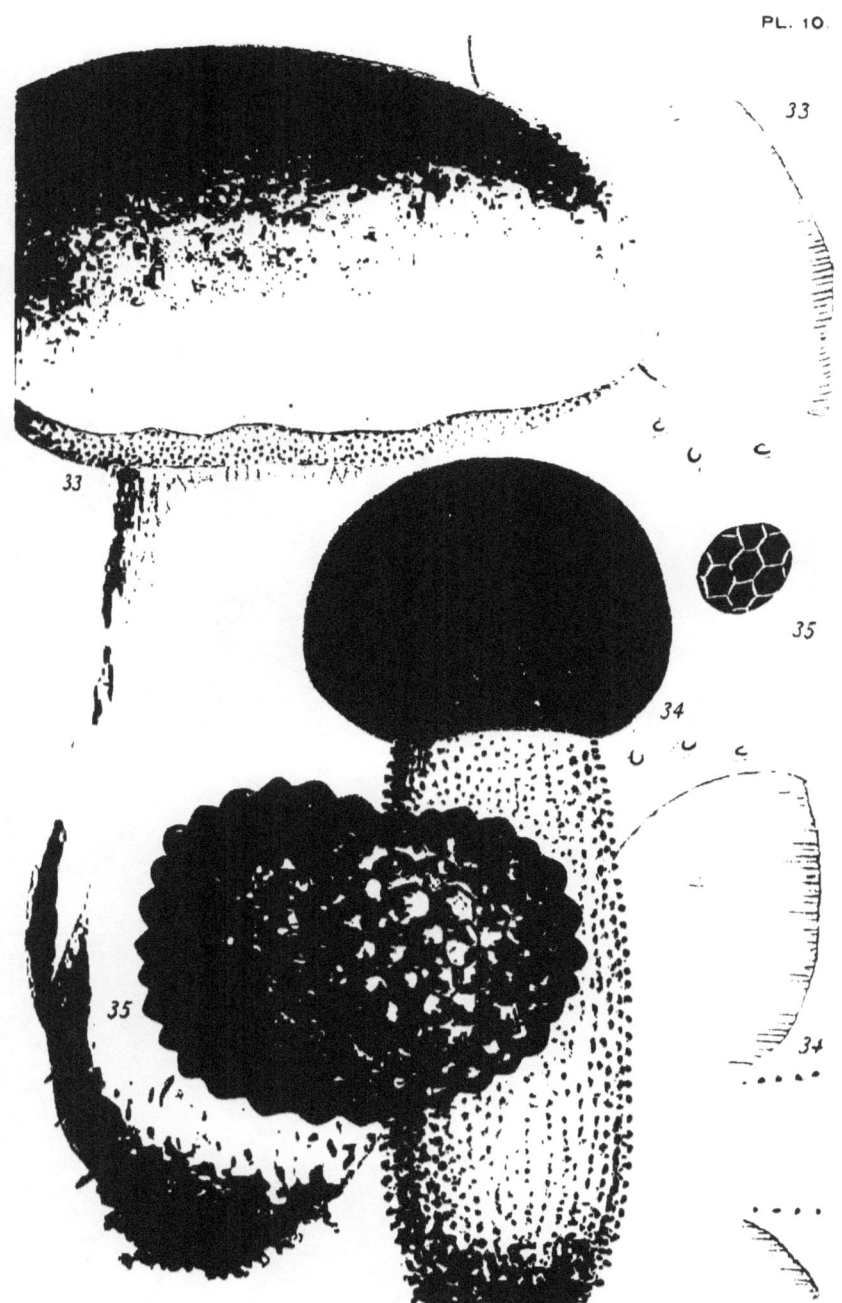

33

33

35

34

35

34

XXII.—FRAGRANT MUSHROOMS.

A CURIOUS question has been asked, but as yet received no satisfactory reply, as to what is the special purpose which is served by the odours of mushrooms, and especially those in which the odour is fragrant and pleasant. Are they designed to be attractive? and if so, of what? And are they in any way associated with the perpetuation of the species? At present we know nothing for certain of the fecundative element in the mushroom tribe, and consequently of fertilization, or cross fertilization, or hybridity, and so all we can do is to speculate and dream. Still the fact remains that certain fungi have odours peculiar to them, and two or three of these come within the range of our present object.

The particular odour alluded to by the term " fragrant mushrooms " is very different from the faint mouldy odour which is not uncommon in fungi of the mushroom type, or even of that strong and peculiar odour of meal which is characteristic of many edible species. This odour, which has good title to be called fragrant, is of the coumarine type. Something not unlike the Tonquin bean, or melilot, or new mown hay, or, as some call it, of anise. It seems that the sense of smell differs in individuals, as does

K

the sense of taste, and this is well exemplified in the different opinions which different people are in the habit of expressing as to the peculiar odours of fungi. Present the same specimen to half a dozen individuals by way of experiment, and no two of them will express the odour in the same terms. This renders it the more difficult for us to describe odours, which should be inhaled to be correctly appreciated.

Sweet odours are not at all common in fungi, but the "green, sweet mushroom" (*Agaricus odorus*) is one of the exceptions. It is always more or less fragrant, and always the same odour, whether fresh or dried, and is usually called an odour of anise. The little species which is its possessor is to be found in woods, growing amongst dead leaves, and seldom more than three or four at a time, often only one or two. The odour is rather strong and fascinating; when once inhaled there is a persistent inclination to keep sniffing at it, and, fortunately, the agaric is not fragile, but bears the handling exceedingly well. In drying the odour does not disappear, but perhaps rather to increase. The cap of this agaric is usually about an inch and a half or two inches in diameter, thin in the flesh, and of a peculiar dull bluish green, which it is difficult to imitate. It is something of a dull peacock green, approaching verdigris green, but not exactly either, quite smooth, but never viscid or shining, and with the texture of a good kid glove. The stem is short and white, about as thick as a pipe

stem, but hardly two inches long, sometimes not
more than one. The gills are rather broad, attached
to, and a little inclined to run down the stem; they
are not white but of a greyish or ashy tint. It has
been several times figured in books, but in most cases
as a failure, for there is a subtlety about the colour
which seems to evade the artist. Of the odour, however, there is no mistake, and will at any time prove
sufficient for its identification.

There is another similar species, with a greyish cap,
becoming dirty white, but it is so rare that it has
only been recognized in Britain on two occasions. It
is equally fragrant (*Agaricus Trogii*) and equally good
eating.

The other fragrant species to which a special
attention should be directed is by no means uncommon amongst grass in woods in the autumn. It
is the most common of the fragrant species, but is,
unfortunately, very small (*Agaricus fragrans*); the cap
is not more than an inch in diameter, often less, but
it seldom grows alone; where one is found you may
expect to find twenty. The odour is almost identical
with that of the green, sweet mushroom, but hardly so
strong. It also is of a dry, tough texture, and may be
flattened and placed in a pocket-book, so that for
a long time the opening of the book allows the odour
to escape. The cap is convex, almost hemispherical,
with a dimple at the top, but it rarely becomes funnel-
shaped; its colour when quite dry is creamy white,

but it readily absorbs moisture and then it is darker ; the stem is slender, rather long for the size of the cap, say two inches, or more, and of the thickness of a straw. The gills are rather close together, arched, and a little running down the stem, nearly white, paler than the cap. There are two or three species to be found growing in woods which resemble this in size and appearance ; but the nose will always detect the true species without fail.

Should it ever happen that sufficient specimens can be collected to furnish a dish of fragrant mushrooms no one should omit the opportunity, because although there is a certain amount of toughness and dryness about them when fresh, they become tender enough when cooked with any ordinary amount of care. There is one very strong point in their favour, that the most complete novice may be quite sure of being correct in his determination if he will only trust to his nose. There is nothing in the fungus world with that same odour which would do him harm. There is a tough woody fungus to be found growing on willow trunks which has a fainter share of the same odour, but if the novice can get his teeth into that he may be forgiven for all the harm it will do him.

No special instructions are requisite for these small agarics, they may be stewed or fried, and put upon sippets of toast. We should prefer the plan already recommended in other cases—to lay them in a plate with pepper, salt, and butter, and cover with an inverted basin, then place in an oven for ten minutes, and keep covered until placed on the table, when the odour will be quite appetizing enough to make the gourmet wish that the supply had not been so scanty. As a friend once observed—" I am always vexed that I cannot obtain sufficient of them to satisfy me."

This introduction of the subject of fragrant mushrooms suggests allusion to two or three other species which are characterised as edible, but we imagine not particularly digestible. They are not so redolent with the odour as the smaller species, but there is a suggestion of the same odour, or nearly so, which is at least pleasant. One of these supplementary species is called *Lentinus cochleatus*, which is found usually in the hollows of rotten stumps. There is a branched stem deeply buried in the wood, each branch of which bears a cap of somewhat irregular or contorted fan shape, suggesting the tree loving species of the oyster mushroom kind, but with this difference that it is tougher in texture, becoming quite hard when dry, and the edge of the gills are toothed or saw-like, as though they had been gnawed by some insect. There is a peculiar reddish tint throughout the whole cluster, caps and stem, both within and without, the caps being sometimes two or three inches broad. The pinkish-white gills run downwards on the stem. It is not at all a common fungus, and its chief interest consists in the faint anise-like odour which pervades it. We never felt any inclination to test its qualities as an esculent, on account of its toughness when fresh, and no previous writer in English upon edible mushrooms has ever condescended to notice it, and yet it has been eaten on the Continent. All inquiries amongst our fungus eating friends have failed to discover anyone who has made the experiment.

There is yet another group of tough and rather leathery fungi, at least when old, but somewhat more succulent when young, amongst which is a similarly fragrant species. This is *Panus torulosus*, a clean and rather handsome species with caps two or three inches in diameter, of a pale ochraceous flesh colour, depressed in the middle so as to be almost funnel shaped, and smooth, without any scales, but with a dull, almost velvety appearance ; the stems are one-sided, and short and woolly, especially about the base, with a grey down. The gills are flesh coloured at first, but become more tawny with age, gradually attenuated behind, so as to run down almost like lines upon the stem. This species dries readily when mature, and as it contains so little water, does not shrink or alter its shape, so that it can be kept for years almost of the same colour and condition as when gathered. This fact would suggest that as an edible species it is without promise, and yet some of the continental mycologists contend that it is edible— *when young*. It is a saving clause to allude to its juvenility, for when mature, one would almost as soon think of experimenting upon an old pair of kid gloves as a well grown specimen of *Panus torulosus*. We have not the remotest intention of recommending it either stewed or baked, although it might be as harmless as saddle flaps, and possessing a far more pleasant and attractive odour than *Polyporus squamosus* which was figured by us in a former work on this subject as eaten abroad, but of which Mrs Hussey declared—" One might as soon think of eating saddle-flaps." It seems strange to us islanders that such things as these should ever have been recommended, when we possess some eighty or a hundred species which are at least succulent and juicy and more than half of them excellent. But we Britishers are allowed to possess "insular prejudices."

XXIII.—MORELS.

MORELS have such a singular appearance, and differ so much in structure from the fungi already enumerated, that we must at once endeavour to convey some idea of their general character for the benefit of those who may not have this preliminary knowledge. The whole plant consists of a cap and stem, as in the agarics, but it is a different kind of cap and stem, so different as to puzzle the uninitiated. The cap is globose, or oval, or conical, deeply pitted on the outside with deep, angular, hexagonal, or elongated pits or hollows, so as to present a kind of honeycombed appearance. In colour mostly tawny or smoky brown. The base of the cap in some of the species is grown to the stem ; in others it is free from the stem half way up. The inside of the cap is hollow and continuous with the hollow of the stem. The latter is mostly robust, either about as long as the height of the cap, or it may be several times longer, mostly even, but very hollow, so that nowhere is the flesh thicker than about the eighth of an inch.

The whole outside of the cap is a spore bearing surface, but the spores are not naked as in agarics or boleti, but usually eight spores are produced in a row within a long, thin, cylindrical membrane, called a spore-sac or ascus. These sacs, or asci, are closely packed side by side, and immersed in the flesh of the cap. When the spores are ripe the sac opens at the apex and the spores escape. The same kind of spore system is also found in the helvellas, hereafter alluded to. The whole substance of these fungi is rather dry, but fragile, and not in any degree fibrous or tough. They have an odour resembling that of mushrooms, and a sweet, pleasant taste. As far as we are aware, all the known species are edible.

Morels are commonly exposed for sale about the month of June in the Parisian markets ; but they are rarely exhibited, even in Covent Garden, in this country, although the dried fungus can generally be purchased, if enquired for, throughout the year, chiefly being imported.

The common morel (*Morchella esculenta*) has a rather globose cap, about two inches in diameter, attached to the stem at the base, this latter being about the length of the height of the cap, and half an inch thick. The stem is white and the pileus of a tawny grey. It is found in spring or early summer, say from the latter end of April to June, on chalky or clayey soil, rarely on sand, and sometimes on burnt ground. It is not unusual to find it in old double hedgerows and occasionally in woods and orchards.

The conical morel (*Morchella conica*) is nearly of the same size, but the cap has a conical shape, is almost twice as long as broad, and the pits on the cap are long and narrow, with here and there transverse veins. Otherwise it so much resembles the common morel that some persons believe it to be only a variety of that species. At any rate it is equally delicate, and that is of the greatest importance to us.

There is yet another species, with a rather conical cap, but the bottom edge of the cap is free from the stem, and for half way up. It is smaller in the cap, and longer in the stem than the conical morel, and, from the half free pileus, or cap, has been called the free-cap morel (*Morchella semilibera*). It occurs at the same period of the year, and in similar stations to the other species. It seems strange that in many parts of the country the rural population appear to have no name and no knowledge of these fungi, and yet they are about the safest and most delicious of the entire tribe.

There are two other, much larger, but we fear much rarer species, which deserve a place in this enumeration. The one species is the great morel (*Morchella gigas*) which has often a stem six inches long and two to three inches thick. The cap is also rather conical, free at the edge, and half-way up, two or three inches high and broad. It resembles a gigantic form of the last species, but differs from it not only in size, but also in the scaly stem. It has only been found a few times in this country.

The other, and last, species is Smith's morel (*Morchella Smithiana*) which was at first mistaken for the giant morel or the thick-stemmed morel, and so called when figured in the *Journal of Botany*. The cap is subglobose, tawny, and with deep large pits, the base continuous with the stem. It reaches to a foot in height and seven inches in diameter, with a robust stem. Several instances are known of its occurrence in this country and a single specimen is quite sufficient for a substantial meal. It is remarkable how very persistently a certain class of people, presumably with toes more active than their brains, make war upon unknown fungi, kicking them in pieces, without thought or reason, whenever met with. On one occasion the remains of a splendid specimen of this morel, the size of a half quartern loaf, were found kicked about by some boys, and brought to us for identification. It was a lamentable wreck, but when carefully washed made an excellent meal.

There are at least two other rare species which are British, but we fear too rare to be a trustworthy source of food supply.

Before adverting to culinary processes it may be remarked that if morels are sprinkled with salt, and treated in the same manner as mushrooms are treated for " Catsup," they will yield a delicate, almost colourless liquid sauce, of the same nature as " Catsup," but for which we presume some special name must be invented, and registered, as it has not the same flavour, and with the same name would be liable to misconception.

Morels are cooked in various ways, according to individual taste. For a *ragoût* the fungi are cleaned and wiped to remove all trace of sand, cut in two, then placed in a stewpan with butter, and set over a clear, brisk fire ; when the butter is melted, squeeze in a little lemon juice, give a few turns, and add salt, pepper, and a little grated nutmeg. Cook slowly for an hour, adding at intervals small quantities of beef gravy or jelly broth. When done, thicken with yolk of eggs.

Another method consists in washing and wiping the morels (which should never be omitted), then put them on the fire with butter, salt, pepper, and a small bundle of herbs. Simmer together, and add a little flour ; soften with good beef gravy. Let them cook, and reduce, over a gentle fire, then remove the bundle of herbs. Fry some bread crumbs in butter, then beat up the yolks of three eggs, add a pinch of powdered sugar which mix with the morels, and pour the whole over the fried bread crumbs previously put in a dish.

The Italian method consists in cutting the morels into two or three pieces, and putting them in a stew-pan over a lively fire ; add olive oil, pepper, salt, and a bundle of herbs, let them simmer some minutes, then add chopped parsley, a little onion, and a chive of garlic. Continue the cooking over a gentle fire. Soften with beef gravy and a glass of white wine. Serve with a piece of lemon, and bread crumbs fried brown and crisp.

In simpler ways some think that no better plan can be found than to surround a joint of veal with morels and cook them together. It will be remembered that they will dry readily in a current of air, and in this manner keep through the winter, for seasoning and flavouring broths, soups, and stews.

The culture of the morels has scarcely been taken seriously into account, and yet it is one of the possibilities, if an announcement made by M. Simar[1] is to be taken into account. He says—" I brought to

[1] Bulletin de la Societe D'Horticulture de Meaux (1874) p. 7. *Gard. Chron.*, Jan. 8, 1876, p. 43.

the meeting, in January 1872, a pot of arum garnished with large morels, and I had them in like
manner on almost all my pots. After long searching
I came to suspect that it proceeded from the composition of the earth which I used for potting; nevertheless, I could not be positively certain of it. At
the beginning of the autumn of 1873 I made a
composition of earths analogous to that which I had
made in 1872, and obtained exactly the same results.
I am now therefore assured of the culture of the
morel, and that it can be effected with much greater
economy, and less trouble, than the culture of the
mushroom.

"My earth for the purpose is thus composed—(1)
one quarter of two year old tan, well rotted; (2) one
quarter of heath mould or leaf mould; (3) one quarter
of ordinary vegetable mould; (4) one quarter of fresh
loam."

A writer suggests the addition of a fifth proportion
of mould from some spot where the morel is known
to thrive.

M. Simar directs that the whole is to be carefully
mixed together. When the composition is made,
you refill your pots with this fresh compost. At the
beginning of October you make a bed of fresh tan,
in the state it comes from the tanner's hand, six or
seven inches deep, the fresher the tan the better. In
this you set the pots as close together as possible,
and let them remain without touching them; in three

weeks or a month you will find mycelium on the surface of each pot; about three weeks afterwards it disappears. There is no occasion to be alarmed, for five weeks after its disappearance you will find on all your pots hundreds of morels of the size of pins' heads; you have then only to give frequent sprinklings with soft water. The most suitable temperature is 47° F. at the beginning of the culture, and 50° towards its close.

In the autumn two or three excellent substitutes for the morel may be found not uncommonly in our woods. We have witnessed them by scores in Epping Forest, growing undisturbed, for hundreds of Bank Holiday visitors have not the remotest idea of their gastronomic value. The white helvella (*Helvella crispa*) is two or three inches high, almost entirely white, with a fluted, irregular stem, more than half an inch thick, and a twisted, contorted cap, smooth on both sides, not much thicker than brown paper, and about two inches across. No description would give so good an idea of its appearance as a figure (plate 12, fig. 42), for it would be difficult to describe the convolutions of its flexile cap. For the benefit of the botanical student we may add that it is allied to the true morels, and has its spores contained in asci, packed side by side in the flesh of the upper surface of the cap. It is amusing sometimes, when the spores are ripe, to see them jerked out in little white clouds from the surface of the cap, either under the influence of the light, or from the slight touch of a passing object. During September and October it is unusual to pass through a wood without seeing one or two of them, seldom more, by the wayside. There is nothing else like them, so that there is no fear of danger.

When fresh they have a pleasant nutty flavour, but no appreciable odour. Unfortunately a day's excursion seldom furnishes more than a few specimens, but it is always commendable to secure every one, and if sufficient cannot be collected for a ragoût, one or two may be easily dried, and added to the store for the winter.

There is another species, not usually so common, but apparently rather more gregarious in its habits (*Helvella lacunosa*), almost of the same size, and found in similar places. The cap is of dark slaty smoke colour, in Epping Forest sometimes as large as a child's fist, twisted and convoluted so as to differ but little except in colour.

In one spot, a few yards square, in Monk's Wood, we remember on one occasion to have collected a large basket full in half an hour, and subsequently to have usually found a few specimens every year near the same spot. On that memorable occasion we indulged in the good natured folly of introducing this fungus to a mycophagous companion. The result was more gratifying to him than to us, for he is now in the habit of making clandestine visits annually to this spot, in search of the coveted delicacy, and is generally successful. Once seen, it is easily recognised, and once eaten, not readily forgotten.

Passing allusion may be made to a much smaller species, with a slender stem, varying from the thickness of a straw to that of a tobacco pipe, and a cap under an inch in diameter (*Helvella elastica*) ; the whole plant is of a dirty white colour, the cap less lobed, and deformed, and the stem smooth, without any grooves or channels. It is difficult to obtain sufficient for a dish at any time, but solitary specimens may often be gathered and dried. In fact, all the three species may be mixed together, as their flavour is almost identical, [and whether eaten fresh or dried, may be used indiscriminately. It is unnecessary to add that should fortune favour the collector, the same methods of cooking which are employed for morels may be adopted with the helvellas. We have not attempted to invent or suggest any more vulgar name for these "false morels ;" and we fear that they will not soon acquire one for themselves, as they are not obtrusive in their colour or habits, and are not plentiful enough to excite the curiosity of conventional travellers.

36

37

37

39

38

38

XXIV.—TRUFFLES.

IF any fungi merit the title of aristocratic it must be truffles, whether considered in relation to their market value or the uses to which they are applied. The poor man may enjoy his "vegetable beefsteak" or his "vegetable sweetbread," and even indulge in "procerus pie" or stewed "hedgehog," but he is innocent of the flavour of truffles, and does not regale himself with *pate de fois gras*. In former times the hunting for truffles was a branch of industry practised in Sussex and Kent, but in these degenerate days truffle-hunting is almost unknown, and native truffles rarely seen. Possibly as many truffles as ever lie concealed beneath the surface of the Downs, but to collect them is an occupation which does not pay, and our supplies are derived from France. The French truffle has the credit of possessing a superior flavour, and can be supplied at a lower price. At any rate there are people to be found who prefer, or seem to prefer, anything of foreign origin to a like article of native produce.

Truffles are subterranean fungi which grow and perfect themselves beneath the surface of the soil, and give no indication of their whereabouts. They have the appearance of irregular, black, warty no-

dules, sometimes nearly as large as the fist, at others
not exceeding that of a walnut. The interior is
pallid and mottled, the darker spots indicating
cavities filled with the blackish spores. Hunting for
mushrooms is comparatively easy, for the object of
search is visible when present, but truffles might be
plentiful, two or three inches beneath the surface, and
not be visible, or give any sign of their presence.
The only method available in such cases is to find some
animal which instinct or appetite might prompt to
scent out the buried treasure, and mark its hiding-
place. Two kinds of animals have been trained for
this purpose—truffle dogs in our own country and
truffle pigs in France. In both cases the odour of
the truffle is sufficient for the keen scent of the
animals, whilst the human hunter profits by the
produce. These are the instructions—"You must
have a sow, of five months old, a good walker, with
her mouth strapped up, and for her efforts recom-
pense her with acorns; but as pigs are not easily led,
are stubborn, and go astray, and dig after a thousand
other things, there is but little to be done with them.
Dogs are better; of these select a small poodle."
Another writer says of truffle hunting in France:
"A sow is employed to search for the truffles. At
the distance of twenty feet she scents the truffles and
makes rapidly for the foot of the oak where she finds
them, and digs into the earth with her snout. She
would soon root up and eat her treasure were she

not turned aside by the light stroke of the stick on her nose, and given an acorn or a dry chestnut, which is her reward."

A writer on dogs has given the following interesting account of the truffle dog, now almost a rarity. He says that "The truffle dog is a small poodle (nearly a pure poodle) weighing about fifteen pounds. He is white, or black and white, or black, with the black mouth and under lip of his race. He is a sharp, intelligent, quaint companion, and has the homing faculty of a pigeon. When sold to a new master he has been known to find his way home for sixty miles, and to have travelled the greater part of the way by night. They are mute in their quest, and should be thoroughly broken from all game. These are essential qualities in a dog whose owner frequently hunts truffles at night,—in the shrubberies of mansions protected by keepers and watchmen, who regard him with suspicion. In order to distinguish a black dog on these occasions the hunter furnishes this animal with a white shirt, and occasionally also hunts him in a line. They are rather longer on the leg than the true poodle, but they have exquisite noses, and hunt close to the ground. On the scent of a truffle (especially in the morning or evening, when it gives out most smell) they show all the keenness of a spaniel, working their short cropped tails, and feathering along the surface of the ground for from twenty to fifty yards. Arrived at the spot where the fungus lies buried some two or three inches beneath the surface, they dig like a terrier at a rat's hole ; and the best of them, if left alone, will disinter the fungus, and carry it to his master. It is not usual, however, to allow the dog to exhaust himself in this way, and the owner forks up the truffle, and gives the dog his usual reward—a piece of bread or cheese ; for this he looks, from long habit, with the keen glance of a Spanish gipsy. The truffle hunter is set up in business when he possesses a good dog ; all he requires besides will be a short staff, about thirty inches long, shod with a strong iron point, and at the other end furnished with a two-fanged iron hook. With this implement he can dig the largest truffle, or draw aside the briers or boughs in copse wood to give his dog free scope to use his nose. He travels usually thirty or forty miles on his hunting expeditions, and with this (to use a business term) inexpensive plant, keeps a wife and children easily. We know personally one blue grizzled dog, of the old truffle breed, which supports a family of ten children. The truffle dog is a delicate animal to rear, and a choice feeder. Being continually propagated from one stock he has become peculiarly susceptible of all dog diseases, and when that fatal year comes round which desolates the kennel in his quarter, many truffle hunters are left destitute of dogs, and consequently short of bread ; for they will not believe (as we believe) that any dog with a keen nose and lively temper may be taught to hunt and find truffles. The education of the dog commences when he is about three months old. At first he is taught to fetch a truffle, and when he does this well and cheerfully, his master places it on the ground, and slightly covers it with earth, selecting one of peculiar fragrance for the purpose. As the dog becomes more expert and keen for the amusement, he buries the truffle deeper, and rewards him according to his progress. He then takes him where he knows truffles to be abundant, or where they have been previously found by a well broken animal, and marked. Thus he gradually learns his trade, and becomes (as his forefathers have been for many generations) the bread winner for his master and his master's family; unless he is so fortunate as to become *attaché* to some lordly mansion, or possibly to a royal palace, in which case he is a fortunate dog indeed."

In 1860 it is recorded that a truffle was found in Germany which weighed one pound seven ounces, whilst Wallroth writes of them as having been found formerly weighing two pounds each.

Experiments in truffle cultivation have often been made in France. In the South they are said to be raised by watering the soil with water in which the skins of truffles have been rubbed. In Vaucleuse crops have been raised in a meadow manured with truffle parings; and there also seedling oaks have been reared for the production of truffles at their roots, under the name of oak truffles. M. de Gasparin visited and reported upon one of these truffle grounds. "Encouraged," he says, "by the high price of truffles, the proprietor of a somewhat stubborn soil determined to convert it into a truffle ground. The land was sown with the acorns of the common oak and of the evergreen oak. In the fourth year three truffles were found, and in about four years more upwards of thirty pounds were collected." When he visited the plantation upwards of two pounds of truffles were gathered in a very poor part of the plantation within an hour. All the truffles were taken at the base of the evergreen oaks, but other plantations in Vaucleuse produce them at the foot of the common oak. It has been remarked that the truffles produced about the roots of the common oak are larger and more irregular in form than those of the evergreen oak, which are nearly always spherical.

The truffles are gathered at two periods of the year. In May white truffles are found which never blacken, and have no odour; these are dried, and sold for seasoning. The black truffles are dug up a month before, and a month after Christmas, when they have become hard and acquired all their perfume.

The English truffle is called *Tuber æstivum*, and one of its peculiarities is that the large spores, which are oval, and nearly black, have an outer transparent coat which is divided into deep pentagonal cells, like honeycomb. The French truffle, on the contrary (*Tuber melanosporum*), has brown oval spores covered with rigid spines. Any fragment of either species may at any time be determined by the microscope, so that it can always be decided whether the truffle be the English or the French species. Although the latter have a rather disagreeable odour, the flavour is said to be so much superior that the French has superseded the English truffle in our own markets. The French truffle above alluded to is the Perigord truffle.

Of all British mycologists the one who paid most attention to, and was the greatest authority upon truffles, was the late Mr C. E. Broome, and from a communication of his we have gleaned the following notes. Four species are named as exclusively in use in France. *Tuber melanosporum*, *T. brumale*, *T. aestivum*, and *T. mesentericum*, of which two, or perhaps three, occur in Great Britain. *Tuber aestivum* is apparently the only species to be met with in a recent state in our shops. *T. mesentericum* may at times occur, but it has not yet been noticed there. *T. brumale* has hitherto been found in England of too small a size to be worth sending to market. In Italy there are other kinds, one of which, *T. magnatum*, commands a higher price than any other; and in the southern parts of Italy, Sicily, Syria, and Africa, another species, *Terfezia leonis*, is of common use as an article of food.

The soils in which edible truffles are found in France are always calcareous, or calcareous clays. *T. mesentericum* occurs, however, in ferruginous sands, as is also the case with another species, *Hydnotrya Tulasnei*, which, or a closely allied kind, is largely eaten in Bohemia, under the name of Czerwena Tartoffle.

Some persons have supposed that these fungi are parasitic on the roots of trees. This the Tulasnes deny, and so also does Mr Broome. Some trees appear, however, to be more favourable to the production of truffles than others. Oak and hornbeam are especially mentioned, but, besides these, chestnut, birch, box, and hazel are alluded to. Old truffle hunters in this country usually obtained them chiefly under beech, and in mixed plantations of fir and beech. It would seem that three or four months suffice for their development. They are said to be about as large as grains of millet in the beginning of October, and must acquire their full size before the end of December.

Many attempts have been made to subject these fungi to a regular system of culture, but hitherto almost without success. Borch and Bornholz state that a compost was prepared of pure mould and vegetable soil, mixed with dry leaves and sawdust, in which, when properly moistened, mature truffles were placed in winter, either whole or in fragments, and that after the lapse of some time small truffles were found in the compost. The most successful plan consisted in sowing acorns over a considerable extent of land of a calcareous nature, and when the young oaks had attained the age of ten or twelve years, truffles were found in the intervals between the trees. This process was carried on in the neighbourhood of Loudun, where truffle beds had formerly existed, but where they had long ceased to be productive. In this case no attempt was made to produce truffles by placing ripe specimens in the earth, but they sprang up of themselves, from spores probably contained in the soil. The young trees were left rather wide apart and were cut for the first time about the twelfth year from the sowing, and afterwards at intervals of from seven to nine years. Truffles were thus obtained for a period of from twenty-five to thirty years, after which the plantations ceased to be productive, owing, it was said, to the ground being too much shaded by the branches of the young trees, a remedy for which might have been found by thinning out the trees; but this would not be adopted till all the barren tracts had been planted.

The Messrs Tulasne think that truffle cultivation in gardens can never be so successful as this so called indirect culture, but they think that a satisfactory result might be obtained in suitable soils by planting fragments of mature truffles in wooded localities, taking care that the other conditions of the spots selected should be analogous to those of the regular truffle grounds ; and they recommended a judicious thinning of the trees and clearing the surface from brushwood, &c., which prevents at once the beneficial effects of rain and of the direct sun's rays. It is added that this species of industry has added much to the value of certain districts of Loudun and Civray, which were previously comparatively worthless, and has enriched many of the proprietors who now make periodical sowings of acorns, thus bringing in a certain portion of wood as truffle grounds each year.

Mr Broome was informed by one of the truffle hunters that whenever a plantation of beech, or beech and fir, was made on the chalk districts of Salisbury Plain, after the lapse of a few years truffles were produced, and that these plantations continued productive for a period of from ten to fifteen years, after which they ceased to be so.

Should horticulturists be tempted to try their skill in the artificial production of these fungi, they should bear in mind the conditions most suitable to their nature. They might succeed, for instance, in producing them in filbert-plantations, or in gardens thickly set with fruit trees ; and they should plant mature specimens in well trenched ground, on a calcareous substratum, and be careful not to stir the soil to any depth till the autumn or winter of the following year,

in order not to disturb the mycelium ; and it would
be well perhaps, in case they find a successful result,
not to take too largely of the crop the first year or
two, but to give them time to establish themselves
thoroughly in the locality. It would seem, however,
that when once established, deep stirrings of the soil
would tend rather to encourage than to check their
increase, as giving the mycelium a lighter soil in
which to vegetate, and preventing the growth of roots
of surrounding trees, &c.

Imported truffles, in addition to those which are
received in the fresh state, are either in dried slices,
which are in least esteem, or the whole or segments
of the fresh truffles preserved in oil, and sold in
bottles.

A spiny spored truffle is also recorded as British
(*Tuber brumale*), and it is found in some parts of
France, but does not appear to be held in great
esteem. In England it only makes its appearance
occasionally, and as a rarity.

The red truffle of Bath (*Melanogaster variegatus*)
is almost traditional as a truffle substitute. It is said
that formerly it was sold as a truffle in the markets
of Bath, but we can find no trace of it in such a
capacity now. It is still a British species, and although it is a subterranean species, it is not a true
truffle. The spores in truffles are produced within
broad membranous sacs or asci, and are therefore
what is termed ascigerous, and allies of the great

group of *Sphæria*. The red truffle has naked spores,
produced in cavities of the fungus, free, and not enclosed in asci. These latter are therefore allied to
the puff balls, and are in fact subterranean puff balls.
They are of a brownish colour, irregularly globose,
small and smooth, found usually in the ground at the
foot of beeches, in the south of England. The naked
spores are small and dark coloured. No one in this
generation appears to have any knowledge of the
Melanogaster, either as a "red truffle" or as an
esculent.

Truffles are such an old and aristocratic delicacy
that it must be expected to learn that the methods of
preparing them for the table are exceedingly
numerous. The Rev. M. J. Berkeley used to affirm
that the very best plan, according to his experience,
was to bury the entire truffle in hot wood ashes, on
an old fashioned hearth, and roast them thoroughly,
When ready for the table they could be divested of
their skins and all the ashes adhering to them. But
there are far more elaborate methods, as we shall
presently show.

For a ragoût the tubers should be well washed, and
afterwards soaked in oil, then cut in slices about a
quarter of an inch in thickness, place in a stewpan,
with oil or butter, salt, pepper, and a little white wine.
When cooked bind the whole together with the yolk
of eggs.

Prepared after the Italian manner, middle-sized

truffles are selected, cut in fine slices, and placed in a stewpan with oil, salt, pepper, parsley, shallots, and chopped garlic. Let them cook gently over a slow fire, and serve with the juice of lemon.

The Piedmontese method varies in soaking them first in oil, then slice them thin, and put them in a stewpan with salt, oil, and pepper, grating over them some Parmesan cheese; then the stewpan should be placed over the hot cinders for a quarter of an hour.

Other and simpler methods have also been recommended—such as wrapping each truffle in buttered paper, and cooking them by steam. Also take the truffles when cleaned and sprinkle them with salt and pepper, then wrap each in several folds of paper, garnished with rashers of bacon. They should be cooked a full hour, then denuded of their paper envelope, wiped, and served hot.

XXV.—HORN OF PLENTY.

ANOTHER prejudice was killed when we first essayed to cook and eat that rather unpromising looking fungus which we call the "Horn of Plenty." In appearance it is not unlike the conventional figure of the Cornucopia drawn in books, and although for many years acquainted with it, having flattened and dried it scores of times, it never occurred to us to eat

it, until a suggestion of its being edible met our eyes
in a foreign book.   Up to then we should have thought
as much of stewing our slippers as *Craterellus cornucopioides*.   When dried it resembles strips of " upper
leather," and, at its best, scarce more inviting than the
thumb of a driving glove.   Appearances in this case
were thoroughly deceptive, and we hasten to make
amends.

This fungus is plentiful on the ground in autumn,
in Epping Forest and the New Forest, but its
structure and scientific position is wholly different
from any others which find a place in this volume.
There are no gills, or pores, or spines, and the surface
which bears the spores is almost smooth.   However,
let us attempt its description.   In shape it is a long
inverted cone, or trumpet, about three inches high,
two or three, or more, generally growing together,
with the thin end in the ground.   At the top it is
about two inches broad, and hollow down to the
bottom, the substance not being thicker than the
" upper leather" of a boot.   The top edge is bent
over all round something like the end of a trumpet,
only more so, but it is flexuous, and lobed or split.
In colour the exposed surface at the mouth, which is
the inner surface of the horn, is a dingy brown, with
darker streaks.   Outside it is almost black, with
a frosty bloom over it, like the " bloom " on a fresh
plum.   This is the surface which bears the spores ; it
is not quite even, but with little shallow depressions,

especially in the upper part. Very gradually attenuated downwards, it is scarcely a quarter of an inch
broad at the base, seldom quite straight, but curved
and bent, sometimes distorted. The fanciful might
call them "fairy trumpets," or "horns of plenty" for
the good folk. Growing on the ground, almost buried
in grass or dead leaves, they are hardly conspicuous,
but as a great number are usually found growing
together, it is not difficult, when once found, to secure
sufficient for a dish. There is no odour that is
appreciable, and what the taste may be in the fresh
state we have never ascertained.

Hitherto we have never departed from our first
method of cooking, which was simple and satisfactory. The "horns" were sliced down the middle
from top to bottom, and carefully washed. On
account of their shape this preliminary is essential,
because the form favours the deposit of sand and
other substances at the bottom of the tube, and
because it obviates the risk of snail, slug, or earwig
making it a hiding-place. When washed and dried,
the pieces are placed in a stewpan with salt and
pepper, and a little water, or, better still, gravy or
stock, but we have been content with water, then
stewed gently till soft, thickened with a little flour,
or with the addition of chopped parsley, if desirable,
and served. The aroma is quite mushroomy during
the process, and the result so satisfactory that we
have never missed an opportunity of gathering them

since. An inveterate fungus eater, who was with us on one occasion when we collected a supply, took the hint for himself and imitated at a distance, with what success may be gathered from the fact that now he thinks nothing of a walk of six or eight miles with the prospect before him of a dish of *Craterellus*.

XXVI.—JEW'S EARS.

THIS name has been applied to several different fungi having some fancied resemblance to ears. In some parts of England the large "ground cups" or *Pezizæ*, and particularly *Peziza venosa*, are called Jew's ear, but the one which has the sanction of age and universality is the *Hirneola*, the Jew's ear of elder stumps not uncommon in this country. It has never been regarded here as an edible fungus, but, in some parts of the world, it has no small reputation in that sense. The scientific name is *Hirneola auricula-Judæ*, which is written down here to show that the cognomen of Jew's ear is present even in the botanical name, and is corroboration of its accurate use in connection with the *Hirneola*. It is rather a gelatinous, flabby-looking, thin, expanded cup, or saucer-like fungus of a brownish colour when fresh, smooth in the inside and veined or plaited, so as to have some resemblance to a human ear. Outside it is

shortly velvety and greyish olive.   In size it varies considerably from one to three inches, and is attached by a point at the back, out of the centre, often nearly on one side.   When dry it becomes hard and horny, shrinking considerably in the process.   In past times it had its medicinal uses, and, on that account, is included in most of the old herbals, but the reputation of all virtue has left it long ago, and now that all its occupation is gone, it is regarded simply as a curiosity.   Not so, however, in South-Eastern Asia where it still finds favour for the compounding of those gelatinous dishes of which the Chinese are so fond.   Not only is it largely imported, with other species, but one of these is artificially cultivated to supply the demand.

"Mu-esh" is found spontaneously growing on the bark of wild cherry in Central China.   It is a species of Jew's ear (*Hirneola polytricha*), and is also cultivated at Yun-Yang, whence it is exported to all parts of China, being esteemed as an article of food.   It is of great commercial importance, the quantity annually produced being very large.   Small trees of the China oak (*Quercus sinensis*) are cut down and cut into poles about six to ten feet long, and three to six inches in diameter, and left to rot on the ground for a year.   In the following spring, when the wood has become more or less rotten, the poles are erected into shed-like structures, and these stud the sides of the hills in places.   The "mu-esh" comes spontaneously on the bark, and in about two years has grown all over it. After two years the poles become quite rotten and no more mu-esh is produced.

The original source of the Pacific Jew's ear was the small islands of the Pacific and New Zealand, but it is to be found in Australia, New Guinea, and many other places. The seat of the trade is New Zealand, for which the only market is China. It is largely used by the Chinese in soups with farinaceous seeds, and also as a medicine, being highly esteemed. The Chinese have long been in the habit of using another species of this same genus that is indigenous in North China, and also in importing what has been called another species, but really appears to be the same, from other Isles of the Pacific, so that the use of this kind of fungus as an article of food is not new to them.

At first, and for a considerable time, the New Zealand fungus was exported only in small quantities. The demand rapidly increasing, and the article plentiful, and obtained at little cost, save the labour of gathering and drying it, its export rapidly increased.

The price paid to collectors for it was originally small, only one penny per pound, at which figure it remained for some time. It became nominally two pence half penny in some places, which sum is often paid in barter. It is said to be sold in China at the shops after the rate of tenpence per pound, or more, retail. The declared value in the customs returns has ranged from £33 to £53 per ton, which, doubtless, is under the real value.

From 1872 to 1883, or during twelve years, the exports from New Zealand were no less than 1858 tons, valued at £79,752, and in one year, that of 1882, the declared value of the exports was £15,581.

A recent chemical analysis of this fungus in its air-dried condition has shown that it is singularly poor in albuminoid, or muscle-forming substances, and differs remarkably in this respect from the numerous edible fungi previously examined. The chief constituent of what are called the digestible carbohydrates (70 per cent. of which are present) is a gum-like body allied to bassorin. It swells up greatly in water, and is soluble in dilute warm solutions of caustic alkalis. Its solutions gelatinize in cooling. This is the mucilaginous property for which it may be assumed that it is chiefly valued, and which always has a fascination with the Chinese.

A parcel of the dried fungus was sent to the International Exhibition of 1862 from Singapore, as an article of food, but without any definite information. It was the European, and not the Australasian species, but whence derived it is impossible to say; doubtless it had been imported into Singapore for sale to the Chinese.

The other " Jew's ears," above alluded to, known as

such locally, and with little authority, are of very different structure, however similar they may be in appearance. But it requires a strong imagination to assimilate the appearances. The typical form of the species of *Peziza* is that of a cup, so that these are sometimes called "Earth Cups" if they are in the habit of growing on the ground. It is the inner surface of these cups which is fertile and bears the spores, enclosed in long, delicate cylindrical tubes or sacs, termed asci, each of which contains normally eight spores. It is essential to point out this difference in structure, which is more like that of the morels, than that of either the agarics or even the veritable Jew's ears.

The most promising of these cups, from a gastronomic point of view, is the "veined cup" (*Peziza venosa*) which has a strong and rather nitrous odour as it grows old, or begins to dry ; the cups themselves are about two inches in diameter, whitish and mealy on the outside and veined or puckered at the base, the inner surface is of a dark, rather purplish brown. When mature they expand and flatten out a little, but split from the edge downwards in doing so, and then the under surface is but little seen. The thickness of the cup is not greater than the length of one of these printing letters, so that an entire cup is not more than a mouthful, and as the species is not particularly common, it has not much merit as a food product. The disadvantage in nearly all the species

of *Peziza* is that they are comparatively small, taking
the thickness of the flesh into account, and would
scarcely have encouraged us to include them in this
work at all, except in connection with the *Hirneola*,
and then perhaps rather as " curiosities of food " than
as likely to become staple articles.

The "bladdery cups " (*Peziza vesiculosa*) are more
generally common on the ground, rich soil, rubbish,
and manure heaps. The cup is at first globose, dirty
white, about an inch across or more, and granularly
mealy, then it has a small jagged opening, and at
length it is expanded like a cup, but the edge is
usually a little turned in, until it is quite old. When
fully opened it will attain two or three inches, and
the interior is smooth pale brown. This is a widely
dispersed species, being found all over Europe, in
North America, and in Australia and New Zealand.
In comparison with the last species we consider this
inferior for eating, and taking into account the
trouble of collecting and cleaning, it is hardly worth
the pains. We have had this sent to us also under
the name of Jew's ears, which probably is locally
applied indiscriminately to any ear-shaped fungus.

The orange cups (*Peziza aurantia*) is widely known,
because of the bright orange colour of the inside of
the cups, so that it is a most beautiful and conspicuous object. The cups are often three inches, or
more, when fully expanded, and a number of them
will be often found growing together in damp places.

It is whitish on the outside, and thinner in substance than the "bladdery cups," certainly more attractive. This, again, is found all over Europe, in India, across to the United States, and in the southern hemisphere. At times sufficient may be collected for a good dish, and we have seen them placed as decorations on the dinner table instead of flowers, with a very pretty effect. Some may think the result more satisfactory than cooking and eating them. In the latter condition they are delicate, but without much flavour.

There are several other kinds of "cups" which could be eaten, and indeed we doubt if any of the species are unwholesome. Not one has yet had the reputation of being poisonous, or even suspicious or disagreeable. They usually flourish in the autumn, when agarics are plentiful, and no one would be at the trouble of hunting all day for a few cups of *Peziza*, when the basket could be filled with agarics in half an hour.

Whenever it has been our fortune to try them, chiefly out of curiosity, their preparation has been confined to simple stewing; but unless carefully washed beforehand, they are liable to grittiness, which is rather unpleasant to most people.

XXVII.—THE RUSSULES.

IT is very difficult to describe the russules with sufficient precision to enable anyone who is not a mycologist to distinguish them well enough to eat them. Those who are well acquainted with fungi, and have plates to guide them, will sometimes hesitate, and when the question is one of food or poison, there should be no hesitation. There are bright red russules which will produce serious internal disturbance, and induce dangerous symptoms, even if nothing more, and there are others of the same colour which are recommended as edible. The differences are those which a practised eye would detect, but not such as an ordinary fungus eater would recognize; hence very little can be attempted with them in a work of this kind, which is designed for general use.

It may be premised that in the true agarics the long gills traversing the under side of the cap from the stem to the circumference alternate with shorter ones placed between them, whereas in the russules there are, in most cases, only long gills radiating from the stem, without short ones proceeding from the margin inwards, and alternating with them, or, if short gills are present, they join the long gills, or

grow to them at their inner extremity. This seems
in itself a minute and technical distinction, but
practically it produces a recognizable difference of
appearance in the gills. Another feature in the
russules is that they never possess a collar, or ring,
round the stem, and the latter is soft, without any
rigid outside coating analogous to bark. Finally, the
spores are globose, mostly rough, and either white or
pale ochre. Experience may soon enable a person to
distinguish between a russule and an agaric, but a
mere verbal description will hardly accomplish the
feat.

In despite of the initial difficulty, we must attempt
some account of two or three species, even at the risk
of appealing only to those who are able to distinguish
a russule at once. One of the most commendable
species is the sea-green russule (*Russula virescens*)
which generally grows beside paths in woods in the
summer or early autumn, but is nowhere common.
The cap is at first convex, with the margin curved
inwards, from three to four inches in diameter. The
cuticle is whitish, covered with an opaque coating
resembling meal, which gradually cracks and breaks
up, as the cap expands, into a covering of irregular
small angular spots or patches, the thickness of which
varies according to the thickness of the original
mealy coating ; the cracks between the spots show
the white cuticle, but the little patches are sea-green
or yellowish green, or ochre, communicating to the

cap a mealy or mouldy appearance. The stem is short and thick, sometimes contorted by its efforts to push up the cap through a resisting soil, fleshy but fragile and white. The gills are white, very brittle, but usually simple, with here and there one which is forked towards the outer extremity. This is a very distinct fungus, easy of recognition, and gastronomically one of the best. The Italians recommend cooking it on the gridiron, but Dr Badham says that the peasants about Milan are in the habit of putting it over wood embers to toast, eating it afterwards with a little salt, in which way it has a savoury smell and a taste like that of a crab. Although it is said to dry well, it is not one of the best of species for that purpose. With no perceptible odour when fresh, it acquires one in drying, which we confess is rather strong, but we fail to recognize in it any resemblance to salt meat.

Another mild and agreeable species is the pinkish russule (*Russula vesca*) which has a firm convex cap, soon flattened and at length depressed, often veined and streaked. The colour varies, as it does in most of the species, in intensity, but it is generally of a fleshy pink, darkened in the centre, and occasionally suffused with a flush of lilac. The diameter is commonly about three inches, with a firm, solid stem, rather peculiarly reticulated and normally white, occasionally dashed or patched with pink. The gills are white, many of them forked, rather close together, reaching to, and touching the stem. It occurs mostly in open places in woods. One feature in this russule is the firmness of the cap and stem, and another the peculiar pink of the cap, which is darkest, or rather is replaced by a darker colour in the centre, spreading in streaks all around.

The peacock russule (*Russula cyanoxantha*) is in many respects similar to the last, but the cap is shaded with light blue, or peacock blue, and pink or yellow. It might almost be called rainbow russule, with its variable prismatic colouration. In size it is almost the same as the foregoing, but there is more blue or purple in the colour, and the disc or centre of the cap grows pale and yellowish. The stem is quite smooth, even, and white, about two or three inches long ; the gills are broad and rounded behind, many of them forked. The whole substance, and especially the stem, is not so firm as in *R. vesca*. The flesh is white beneath the separable cuticle, whereas in that species it is reddish. The margin of the cap in both species is even, that is, without parallel lines. There is great resemblance between them as esculents, and they grow in similar localities. Perhaps it would be rather difficult for the novice to distinguish one from the other.

It would be useless to add other species less easy of recognition, but equally wholesome, amongst those which have white gills and spores. But there are some in which the gills are more or less yellow, equally good, two of which may be added, and if confounded with each other no harm will be done. The common russule (*Russula integra*) is found in woods throughout summer and autumn. It is mild to the taste, but one of the most variable in colour. The cap is commonly ruddy, sometimes shaded with blue or brown or olive. The cap is fleshy and convex, then becoming flattened and depressed, rather fragile when mature, and covered with a viscid cuticle, which soon loses colour. The margin is indented all round with parallel depressed lines or shallow furrows, with small tubercles in the space between them, but chiefly when in the mature condition. The cap is three or four inches broad, and the flesh white. The stem is commonly stout, short at first, then club shaped, or swollen in the middle, white and spongy. The gills are nearly free from the stem, very broad, not crowded, connected by veins at the base, at first whitish, then yellowish, powdered with the ochraceous spores.

The other species (*Russula alutacea*) is chiefly found in beech woods, and is about the same size as the foregoing; the cap is red or dark purple, becoming pale, especially in the centre, and is also covered with a viscid cuticle. The stem is stout and solid, about two inches long, and equal throughout, even and white, often variegated with red. The gills are at first free from the stem, thick, and very broad, connected by veins at the base, all of them being equal in length, at first pale yellow, then bright ochre but *not* powdery with the spores. Taste mild and pleasant, with a tendency to become acrid when old.

Except in one or two species the russules are deficient in any perceptible odour ; as a rule the gills are tender and fragile, and the stem spongy. Most of them are rather sticky on the cap when moist, and they are not expanded long before they begin to decay. As esculents we have never regarded them with any especial favour, if we except the sea-green russule, and certainly there is nothing to induce a beginner in the art of fungus hunting to risk a mistake. Dr Badham neverthless says that one of the species (apparently the one called by us peacock russule) is an excellent fungus, and he adds that Roques introduced it into the houses of many of his friends, some of whom preferred it to the common mushroom, "an opinion shared by several of our own friends on this side the Channel."

The russules are tender fungi and require very little cooking, but we do not recommend stewing, as they are rather watery, and not strong in flavour. Baking in a covered dish with the usual condiments is the only method we have resorted to, and the best we can suggest. Finally, we caution strongly against experiments with any of the bright scarlet or crimson coloured species, unless determined to be harmless by a competent authority.

XXVIII.—STUMP MUSHROOMS.

THE most common and the most universally eaten on the Continent of all the stump mushrooms is the one which has no favour in this country. In Vienna it is called the stump mushroom and is exposed for sale everywhere. It is always in demand, and yet we consider it tough, bitter, and not at all pleasant. Perhaps it is because we use it differently, for there they only employ it as a kind of condiment, adding a little to all their soups, stews, and made dishes. So common is this fungus with us in the autumn that *Agaricus melleus* is a bye-word and a nuisance. If we could only eat it and recommend it, perhaps we should reduce the number perceptibly, but now it turns up everywhere. No fungus is perhaps more variable in appearance, and it takes a long time to be sure of it under its many phases. It may be premised that it is more or less confined to rotten stumps, and even when it seems to be growing out of the grass it may be concluded that there is some bit of rotten wood buried beneath where it springs. As a rule it forms dense clusters, almost covering the old stump from which it grows. The cap is of a honey-coloured brown, about two inches across, sometimes twice as large, occasionally larger, with a darker centre, more or less scaly or fibrous. The stem is rather long, it may be six

inches, paler than the cap and fibrous, with a large
spreading ring near the top. The gills are dirty
white, and soon discoloured and stained or spotted
with dull red. The spores are white, and so profuse
that grass, wood, dead leaves, or whatever lies beneath
the fungus soon become covered with a coating of the
snow-white spores. This is a feature which cannot
fail to be observed. The whole of the fungus is of a
rather dry consistence, not viscid, but sometimes so
soaked with moisture after rain, that it is scarcely
distinguishable. And this is the ubiquitous *melleus*,
the honey-coloured stump mushroom, common everywhere, and almost everywhere in profusion, but no
one holds it in respect. In this instance "familiarity
breeds contempt;" even slugs and maggots do not
appear to hold it in much esteem. All books on
edible fungi that have been written include this
species, but it would not have found a place here if
such had not been its antecedents, for, although perfectly harmless, it is not such a dainty morsel as one
would recommend to his friends. One of our fungus
eating coadjutors always speaks of it as an "awful
fraud," and therefore we may be excused for omitting
any instructions in its preparation for the table.

Although the "melleus" is not to our liking,
there is another species, confined apparently to old
beech trees and stumps, for which we have better words
to write. The slimy beech caps (*Agaricus mucidus*)
are usually plentiful wherever there are old beeches,

but not elsewhere. They spring in tufts from the bark, and being of an ivory whiteness when the slime is washed away, are conspicuous objects. The cap is usually one or two inches in diameter, but we have seen specimens five or six inches. It is entirely covered, when growing, with a coat of slime, and then is often of a smoky colour, but in Epping Forest and Burnham beeches it is more often ivory white. The stem is rather long and slender, with a broad ring in the upper portion, and usually thickened at the base. The gills are very broad and distant apart ; these and of course the spores also are quite white. The most remarkable feature in this species is the covering of slime, like diluted gelatine, with which the entire fungus is invested, and on this account many persons are prejudiced against it, notwithstanding its elegant and graceful form. Having once tasted it, properly cooked, all such prejudice vanishes.

The flesh of the cap is thin, and the whole fungus small, but it is a delicacy not to be despised. The only method we have adopted with them is to cut off the stems, and place the caps on sippets of toast, with a little pepper and salt, and a small piece of butter on each, cover with an inverted basin, and cook them for ten minutes in an oven. When ready they are very tender and digestible, and of delicate flavour. Preferable to some palates to the stronger and more pronounced flavour of the common mushroom.

Another stump mushroom is found in clusters about the base of old trees and stumps with a coarser appearance and of a larger size. It is uniformly of a reddish brown colour, at times and especially when saturated with moisture as dark as a chestnut. The usual diameter of the cap is two or three inches, smooth, and often cracking when dry. The stem is long and spindle-shaped, six or eight inches, tapering very much at the base, fluted, twisted, and contorted in a variety of ways. The gills are broad and whitish at first, but soon become spotted, and at length almost of the colour of the pileus, but the spores are white. It is known as the spindle-stemmed mushroom (*Agaricus fusipes*), and is not by any means uncommon in the late autumn until after the frosts have set in. No one, be he ever such an enthusiast, would claim for this agaric an attractive or pleasing appearance, and yet it has long had a reputation as an esculent. As for ourselves, we have preferred giving the precedence to other species which are found at the same period of the year, and, generally, it is our impression that it is much more neglected than it would otherwise be if it had not so many rivals. Dr Badham calls it "an excellent fungus," and says it may be stewed or dressed in the same manner as the common mushroom, but the most approved method is to select young specimens only, and pickle the caps for winter use. A rough and ready method is, Cut off the stems and wash the caps, so as to remove any

trace of sand, and lay them on a soft cloth to dry.
Put them when so prepared in wide mouthed bottles,
with a blade of mace, a teaspoonful of peppercorns,
and a teaspoonful of mustard seed in each. Then
cover with the strongest white pickling vinegar boiling
hot. When quite cold they should be closely corked
or tied down, but they will not keep for more than
three months.

XXIX.—THE SPARASSIS.

AMONGST little known British fungi there are many
which are so small that the majority of the natives
might reasonably be excused for never having
observed them, or, even if pointed out to them, for
not manifesting any particular interest in them. It
can hardly be expected that those who are not
personally devoted to the study of fungi, or who are
not sufficiently advanced in their love of Nature to
take interest in all the manifestations of her variety and
power, should trouble themselves about some curious
fungus no larger than a pea, or even as minute as a
grain of mustard seed. But, when the object in
question is as large as a man's head it becomes more
astonishing that it should be wholly unknown to the
average sportsman, or holiday maker, and that it has

N

not acquired for itself even a popular name. Some
excuse may be made when the object is so exceedingly
rare as only to be seen a few times in the course of a
generation; but when it is believed to make its
appearance almost annually, in some place or other,
not wholly unfrequented, there is more ground for
surprise.

The fungus now in question appeals not only to
the curious and the scientific, but also to the stomach
of the lover of good things, as much as would a fine
bunch of asparagus, and yet it is comparatively
unknown. Mr Worthington Smith records the
dimensions of a specimen found at the base of Scotch
firs in Kent a few years ago. It took two men to
carry the box in which it was packed, and the box
afterwards became a spacious rabbit hutch. The
sparassis was very compact, solid, and heavy, it
measured three feet and a half in circumference, stood
ten inches high above the ground, with a solid heavy
base of mycelium for six inches beneath the surface.
It was divided and carried by two persons to
Loughton, in two fish baskets, one basket being
sufficiently heavy for one person to carry with con-
venience. This was no microscopical object which
could be readily overlooked. During one day of a
foray in Hampshire two or three specimens were
found the size of a child's head, but these were
considered small. Twice in one season we have met
with them nine inches in diameter.

Supposing that these details may have aroused sufficient interest to desire further information, we will attempt a description of its appearance. The general outline of form is usually more or less globose, and the colour either a creamy white or a pale ruddy yellow, *not* of the lemon yellow tint, but ochraceous yellow, seeming almost white when growing on the ground. The base consists of a thick rooting stem, the greater part sunk in the ground, arising from a profusion of threadlike mycelium. Upwards the stem is many times divided into numerous branches, which are not visible from the outside. The outer aspect is almost brainlike, consisting of flat laminæ, curled and folded, intricately combined, and twisted, so as to form a dense mass of sinuous folds or plates, the upper portion producing spores on all sides. In decay the whole fungus softens, becomes brownish, and at length settles into a pulpy mass.

The sparassis is either found at the base of trees or on heaths, amongst bracken and heather, something like a large cauliflower denuded of its leaves, and lying upon the ground, no stem being visible. It is often partially concealed, but it seems strange that an object so imposing should so seldom be found except by fungus hunters, and not at all until within the last half of this century.

Of its esculent qualities the accounts are rather barren, except that they are of a high order, which is surprising, since a single specimen is often sufficient for several families. When raw the taste is pleasant, reminding one of a fresh filbert; when cooked, delicate and mild, but scarcely awakening any reminiscences of ordinary mushrooms.

The only suggestions for cooking with which we are acquainted are those given by Roques. The specimens should first be well washed in warm water to clear them from particles of sand or earth, and then drained. Cut into a convenient size, the segments should be baked with butter, parsley, a little eschalot or a fragment of garlic, and seasoned with pepper and salt. When tender, cream and yolk of eggs may be added. During the baking it should be moistened occasionally with a few spoonfuls of broth or gravy. In Austria it is simply fried with butter and sweet herbs, and this primitive plan we have followed for ourselves, whenever good fortune has brought a specimen in our way. Some years since we found one for two or three successive years at the base of the same old tree in Caen Wood, Highgate, and then it appeared no more.

In this connection we may allude to the tremellas, which are not uncommon, but little sought after for the table. Our own experience has been but small, and that not very encouraging. The only species which gave satisfaction was the large pale tremella, which reminds one so strongly of sparassis. This (*Tremella frondosa*), in masses from six to nine inches in diameter, we have found on one or two occasions on the decaying limbs of a tree, or at its base, but only this one individual tree. The description given above of the external appearance of the *Sparassis* would apply equally well to this, except that the stem is entirely absent, the colour of a pinkish yellow, almost flesh-colour, and the texture much softer, and more clammy to the touch. We have not seen it for a quarter of a century, and have but a faint recollection of our then experiences. All we remember was that it was always cooked when found, and eaten by the family with satisfaction, but in what manner it was prepared for the table is now forgotten.

The unsatisfactory experiences relate to the commoner leafy tremella, constantly found on old trunks and branches (*Tremella foliacea*). It is of a smoky brown colour, cold, clammy, and shaky in the hand, in tufts almost the size of the fist, almost of a jelly-like consistence, and by no means inviting. When stewed it resolves itself into a slimy mess which would be acceptible to the Chinese, but not in conformity with English tastes. It is perfectly wholesome, and a little effort might perhaps convert it into a respectable dish by some other process.

Another tremella is to be met with every year on fallen branches and old trunks, which is recommended as edible, but our experiences with the leafy tremella encouraged no experiment. This (*Tremella mesenterica*) is brain-like in its convolutions, gelatinous in texture, averaging in size from that of a walnut to an apple. It is of a very bright orange-red colour, and sufficiently conspicuous, but without any decided odour. As a specimen of a jelly-fungus it is undoubtedly beautiful, but for the table we fear its charms are ephemeral.

These gelatinous fungi approximate perhaps to a vegetable gelatine, and some ingenious manipulator might succeed in producing from them some imitation of table jellies, but the quantity of raw material to be procured is small, and we fear that such energies would be wasted. Water enters so largely into their composition that drying converts them into little shrivelled, hard, horny fragments, like chips of scorched leather.

XXX.—FAIRY CLUBS OR CLAVARIA.

THE observant wanderer cannot but have seen amongst the grass in parks and on lawns some small white or yellow fungi of variable shape, from the simple "fairy club" to the branched and clustered "stag's horn." Commonly only two or three inches in length, and not thicker than a knitting needle, they are conspicuous only by their pure whiteness, or the brilliancy of their golden yellow. Edible they undoubtedly are, perhaps all of them, but so small as to be of little esteem for the table. Sometimes they occur in such plenty that sufficient for a dish may be collected, but it must be a labour of love. The scientific name is *Clavaria*, which has been freely translated as "fairy club," but only a few of them have a club shape, most of the tufted species being very much branched, after the manner of stag's horns. One species only attains a considerable size and preserves the club shape. Some call it the "Hercules club," and it will attain six or seven inches in length, with a diameter of an inch at the apex. In colour it is of a pale yellowish red, almost a ruddy flesh colour, of the tint sometimes called gilvous, solid, and whitish within, growing singly amongst grass ; attenuated gradually downwards, it resembles the conventional form which is given in pictures and statuary to the club of Hercules. But this *Clavaria pistillaris* is not by any means a common fungus, and the collector has to be content with the smaller species. One of the most common in pastures and on lawns is the branched *Clavaria fastigiata*, which is at times so common that a foot can scarcely be set on the ground without crushing it ; so delicate and fragile as hardly to be disentangled from the grass without breaking.

A snowy-white species, with the clubs simple and undivided, grows in similar places, but is often rather rare. This is *Clavaria vermicularis*, of which ten or twenty will form a tuft, and children in some places call them "fairy candles." Much more attractive is a densely tufted and branched species, which we have always met with in woods, rising to three or four inches in height, and of a beautiful amethystine violet, hence it is called *Clavaria amethystina*. This colour is not common amongst fungi, but there is a variety of *Agaricus laccatus* which has a similar tint. More imposing than all are well grown tufts of *Clavaria botrytes*, sometimes forming a bunch as large as a man's fist, with a very thick fleshy stem, as much as one inch thick, which divides upwards into innumerable branches, having the extreme tips tinged with red, whilst the bulk of the fungus is of a creamy white. This is a widely diffused fungus, being found throughout Europe, into Asia, and is not uncommon in Australia. If it were not for the red tips it would resemble a cauliflower without the green leaves, and is considered as good, if not better.

It would hardly avail much to give descriptions, in writing, of all the edible species, since they would be much more easily recognized from drawings, but there is one other common white species which is not unfrequent on hedge banks and grassy slopes. A great number are found growing near each other, but mostly singly, or one or two together. It is peculiar from its irregular club shape and very short wart-like branches and furrowed surface, which has procured for it the name of *Clavaria rugosa*. It is

from two to three inches in length, tapering downwards to a very slender stem.

As articles of food none but the largest are worthy
of much consideration, except as curiosities. It requires some effort to collect sufficient for a dish, and
when obtained and cooked in the most approved
fashion, there is no great compensation in delicacy of
flavour, aroma, or novelty of taste. Many agarics,
to be found with less trouble at the same season,
would give greater satisfaction. There is, however,
one advantage which they possess, and no small one
with timid people, that they are absolutely safe.

XXXI.—MUSHROOM KETCHUP.

KETCHUP, or catsup, for the name is written both
ways, is a sauce prepared from mushrooms, and was
at one time believed to be obtained exclusively from
the common mushroom and the meadow mushroom.
In rural districts, where ketchup making is an annual
autumnal event, the meadow mushroom is preferred
as more highly flavoured. The combination sold in
towns under the name of mushroom ketchup has in
some instances been demonstrated to have been made
without mushrooms at all. It is so easy to detect
spurious mushroom ketchup that it is surprising it

should be attempted. The dark colour of genuine ketchup is due to the dark spores of the mushroom, held in solution, but unchanged in form or colour. A drop of the fluid under the microscope can be challenged instantly as to whether it is mushroom ketchup or not. We need not enquire how the spurious concoction is made, as we have only to deal with the genuine.

It is an error to suppose that good ketchup can only be made from the two mushrooms above named, for we should add also the wood mushroom (*Agaricus sylvaticus*), the two species of *Coprinus* or deliquescent mushrooms (*Coprinus comatus* and *Coprinus atramentarius*), and the two species of viscid Gomphidius (*Gomphidius glutinosus* and *Gomphidius viscidus*). The warted mushroom (*Agaricus rubescens*) and even the common velvety mushroom (*Agaricus velutinus*) may be added to other species. All these are ketchup mushrooms of the first class, but the mushroom gatherers collect almost anything that looks promising, and the Rev. M. J. Berkeley has declared that the mixture of " all sorts " which he has seen consigned to the pot in ketchup manufactories would rather astonish an outsider.

A very simple and effectual method of making this excellent sauce is to wipe the mushrooms and cut off the stems, laying the caps in a pan with the gills upwards, and sprinkling them with salt, taking care to exclude those which are maggoty. They should lie three or four days, and then squeezed with the hand thoroughly so as to extract all the juice. Take one ounce of whole pepper, one ounce of well bruised ginger, and half an ounce of cloves for each pint of the liquor. Boil all together for fifteen or twenty minutes, and when cold, decant into clean bottles, either with or without straining, but, if strained, it is better to add a few peppercorns to each bottle. The corking must be good and well sealed to exclude the air. If at any time afterwards the ketchup shows any tendency to become ropy, it should be boiled again for a short time with a little more spice, when the ropiness will disappear, and it will be as good as ever.

Mrs Hussey recommends a method of ketchup making which retains better the aroma and flavour, by not submitting it to boiling. The mushrooms, being first cleaned from all extraneous matter, and those being utterly rejected which border at all on decomposition, are sliced and salted, and the juice suffered to run off through a colander without squeezing. It is then left for a few hours, and after being decanted carefully from any sediment, placed in small bottles, room being left for a little alcohol in which the proper spices have been previously steeped. Well stoppered, this is said to keep admirably.

The orthodox process of domestic ketchup manufacture is something like the following, modified sometimes to suit individual idiosyncrasies : Mushroom caps, denuded of the stems, are selected, full grown specimens being preferred, and these should be collected in dry weather, and not when the mushrooms are saturated with moisture, in which latter case the ketchup turns musty and will not keep. A layer of mushroom caps are placed, gills upwards, in a deep pan, and sprinkled with salt, some say in the proportion of one ounce of salt to a gallon of mushrooms, and some recommend double that quantity. Then another and another layer of mushrooms are added alternately with salt, until the pan is filled. These are allowed to remain for five or six hours, or all night, and then all the caps are to be broken up and mixed together in a general mess by hand. The pan with its contents should be stood in a cool place for three days, occasionally stirring and mashing so that all the fragments may be well broken and mixed, so as to extract as much of the juice as possible. The liquor may now be poured off, without straining, and measured, so as to add for each quart of liquor a quarter of an ounce of cayenne, half an ounce of allspice, half an ounce of bruised ginger, and two blades of pounded mace. Some prefer to substitute for the cayenne and allspice an ounce of whole pepper and a few cloves. The liquor and the spice is now put into a stone jar, which is covered and plunged in a saucepan of boiling water, set over the fire, and kept boiling for three hours. The contents of the jar may now be turned into a clean saucepan, and allowed to simmer for half an hour. The fluid should then be poured off into a clean jug, and allowed to stand in a cool place until next day. The liquor may then be strained into dry bottles, but the bottles must be clean and dry. Some add a tea-spoonful of brandy to each pint of ketchup.

When bottled, each bottle should be corked and the top covered with resin or sealing-wax to exclude the air. The bottles should be examined from time to time, and, if any ropiness appears, it should be boiled again with a little more spice.

The sediment or refuse of the straining, and all the fragments originally left, may be well squeezed, and the juice obtained boiled down with spice, in the same proportions as above, and will make a rather cloudy but good ketchup for immediate use, but it will not keep.

Double ketchup is made by boiling down good ketchup to half the quantity, which, by evaporating the water, doubles its strength. Some housewives instead of adding brandy to the ketchup put a tea-spoonful of peppercorns in each pint and a half bottle before corking.

For good results mixed fungi should not be used, beyond certain limits ; for instance, although *Coprinus comatus* and *Coprinus atramentarius*, singly or to-gether, will produce a good ketchup, they should not be mixed with the common mushroom, the meadow mushroom, and the wood mushroom, all of which

latter may be combined.   Again, if the warted mushroom (*Agaricus rubescens*) be converted into ketchup,
it should be kept pure and unmixed, because the
resulting fluid will be pale and mild.   The dusky
mushroom (*Agaricus nebularis*) has never been recommended for ketchup, but there is no reason why it
should not be successful, especially as a good supply
of the fungus is probable wherever it is found at all.

It will hardly be possible to make a large supply of
ketchup from the fairy ring champignon (*Marasmius
oreades*), because it is so dry in substance that each
individual will yield but a very small quantity, and,
as the fungus itself is only a little one, an immense
number must be collected to produce a batch.

XXXII.—ABOUT POISONOUS FUNGI.

SEVERAL reasons have influenced us in excluding
descriptions of poisonous fungi from this volume.
Firstly, because they would not assist in obtaining a
knowledge of the edible species, and by error might
be confused with them.   Secondly, because the
popularization of a knowledge of poisons, of any kind,
is never desirable, being liable to do more harm than
good.   Finally, if these reasons have not sufficient
weight, that the dimensions decided upon for this

work, so as to ensure a popular price, would not permit of the introduction of noxious species, without a corresponding diminution in the number of edible species described and figured.

It has always been supposed by the uninitiated that the number of noxious species as compared with the edible is enormous, and are by very far in the majority. Upon investigation this will be discovered to be an error. There are species undoubtedly virulent, which we cannot for a moment deny, but the number of these is much inferior to the number of those which are innocuous, whilst the experience of every year tends to the diminution of the suspected species, many of which have been suspected without any sufficient cause. Select any one hundred consecutive species from a list, and assume that a dozen of them are known to be esculent, hitherto it has been very much the practice to condemn the residual eighty-eight as noxious, which is a cardinal error. There may be a number of species so small that no one would ever enquire whether they were poisonous or not. There would also be a considerable number which might be termed botanical curiosities, species once seen and recorded, but never met with for a quarter of a century, or species so rare that only one or two are met with at intervals. Finally, there will always be a number known to possess some quality other than noxious, such as toughness, deficiency in flesh, &c., which forbids, and always would forbid, their being classed with edible fungi. Ultimately, the known deleterious species would be found diminished to five or six. Indeed we could point out more than a hundred consecutive species in almost any list which would not include a single poisonous species.

Over and over again have we been urged to lay down some rules, or instructions, whereby poisonous may be distinguished from innocuous fungi. As often have we declared, as we do now, that such general instructions are impossible. No rules can be given whereby a poisonous can be distinguished from a harmless species, nothing except knowledge and experience. The poisonous species already known are known because they have a past history which has condemned them, and not from any evidence written upon them. The most experienced mycologist cannot tell by any character, feature, or behaviour, that this or that fungus is poisonous or the reverse. He only knows its antecedents and the company it keeps. A large order of flowering plants, such as the *Solanaceæ*, may be looked upon with suspicion, but the potato and tomato are not poisons. In the *Agarics* the subgenus *Amanita* with warted caps have always been regarded with suspicion because of *Agaricus muscarius* and *Agaricus phalloides;* but two others of the same group, *Agaricus rubescens* and *Agaricus strobiliformis*, are most excellent food. Amongst the *Boleti* it has long been a standing instruction to consider all the species unfit for food, the flesh of which turns blue when cut or wounded. Some of the most virulent turn deep blue when cut, but one or two harmless species turn blue likewise. Again, *Boletus felleus* has the repute of a poisonous species, but it does *not* turn blue when cut. Another bubble is burst, and so every attempt to give general instructions for the discrimination of poisonous and edible species ends in a failure when put to the test.

Although we cannot give patent instructions for general application, we can pronounce cautions, and we do not fail in these cautions from time to time. We caution everyone against experiment in eating fungi which are unknown to them, or not recommended by a competent authority. There are sufficient good and reliable species without making experiments, and, as the only safe guide is knowledge, we recommend everyone to know a few good species thoroughly well, to have them pointed out, to examine for themselves, and then they may always eat them without fear. It is as easy to learn to distinguish one edible species from another as it is to know a partridge from a sea-gull, and yet the latter process requires no man to be an ornithologist.

We have already cautioned readers against agarics with pink or salmon coloured spores, and a caution of this kind may still be continued, even although two species are quite harmless and delicate eating.

Further we may advise abstention from all bright red, scarlet, or crimson agarics or russules unless the

O

individual concerned has most undoubted authority, not merely descriptions in books upon which to rely.

Mushrooms of all kinds pass so rapidly into decay, and consequently suffer rapid chemical change, so that even innocuous species should always be eaten as soon after they are gathered as conveniently may be. Not even the common mushroom is so delicate, or so excellent, at any other period as it is within an hour or two of its being gathered. Certainly no fungus should be cooked as food after it has exhibited any symptoms of decay.

We have known individuals who can at no time eat the ordinary mushroom without inconvenience, and we remember one instance in which only a small fragment of mushroom, eaten accidentally, always produced symptoms of poisoning. This case, and cases of a similar nature, are quite independent of the wholesome nature of the fungus. It is a constitutional idiosyncrasy in the individual which should not condemn the immediate cause. Cases of fungus poisoning are now much more under medical control than formerly, since the method of hypodermic injection of antidotes has been practised, and we have the authority of a physician for stating that he has found it so effectual that he is always prepared to resort to it at once.

Is it true that mushrooms which are under ordinary conditions perfectly good, such as the cultivated mushroom, acquire deleterious properties under certain other unknown conditions? To this we can only reply that it is not only possible, but that it has taken place. We do not pretend to fathom the cause, but can only recognise the fact. It is very rarely that such an experience is heard of, but having really occurred in the past, it is not impossible in the future. There is sometimes to be found in pastures scattered individuals of the ordinary mushroom with a dark brown cap, but in all other respects like the true mushroom. It has come to our knowledge more than once that this dark mushroom is not trustworthy, and should be avoided. What the connection may be between the dark cap and the deleterious property we are not prepared to determine.

Adverting to recognisable features of a general character, we may be permitted to intimate that mushrooms which are mild and pleasant to the taste are so usually edible that we should not hesitate for ourselves to cook and eat any such which came in our way, without credentials. Further, we should always feel suspicious of a fungus with a biting, peppery, or acrid taste, and should not be disposed to eat it, unless its antecedents are in favour of its being perfectly harmless.

There are fungi possessing peculiar rancid, nitrous, or fœtid odours. As we know of none such that are edible, we invariably consider these suspicious, and recommend others to do the same.

If not in themselves poisonous, there are conditions under which otherwise good species may cause inconvenience through bad cooking, by which means they may be rendered indigestible. It is quite possible for mushrooms to be condemned as heavy and indigestible when the fault does not rest with the fungus but with the cook.

In the case of puff balls of all kinds, it is a special injunction that they should not be accepted as good for food after the internal flesh shows the least sulphury tinge. The flesh must always be of a continuous, uninterrupted white.

Undoubtedly fungi which are considered poisonous by us are eaten in Russia, but they have a method of soaking, or preserving, fungi in vinegar, which may serve to explain this anomaly, rather than by attributing it to any climatic conditions. If the poison is of an alkaline nature there is no difficulty in believing that maceration in acid would counteract mischievous effects.

There is much consolation for us who are addicted to fungus eating, on something like scientific principles, that when casualties do happen it is not upon us that they fall. If the records of fungus poisoning are studied, it will be found either that the victims were children, or that they were reckless and stupid, because in so many instances the result has accrued through accepting as mushrooms things which hardly remotely resembled them. Those who eat strange "toadstools" as the result of experience, and the use of their intellect and common sense, being also aware of the danger, consequently escape, and are safe.

XXXIII.—DRIED MUSHROOMS.

FUNGI dried for winter use is a luxury more in vogue on the Continent than with us, and yet the material is as common, and it can only be the taste that is wanting. If the mushroom flavour is desirable during a few autumnal months, why should it not be equally acceptable through the winter? Custom has a great deal to do with these things, and in the present case the custom might be accepted with advantage. The compound sold in some cases as "Mushroom powder" is no equivalent, but rather acts as a deterrent; but genuine mushroom powder is only one of the forms of dried fungi. Under the several species we have notified those which are most suitable for the process of drying, and these may be collected here so as to exhibit at once what are the possible kitchen resources in the winter. It seems strange that at the very period of the year when soups and savoury dishes are most acceptable of all, that such delicate flavourings should be absent. No one who has been in Germany or Austria during winter can fail to have noted the contrast in this particular with home, and not have recognized the "ceps" and dried fungi of other kinds exposed for sale in every street.

This reference reminds us that several kinds of *Boleti* are amongst the most common of the dried fungi. The stem is discarded, the pores cleared away from the under side of the cap, and then the white fleshy cap is cut in slices about the thickness of a penny piece, and thoroughly dried in the air. Certainly *Boletus edulis*, *Boletus scaber*, and *Boletus granulosus*, all of which are described in this work, are common enough, and might be prepared in this manner.

Another fungus which is peculiarly suitable for drying is the fairy ring champignon (*Marasmius oreades*). These can be strung in a line by passing a twine through a hole in the stems, and suspending them in the kitchen until quite dry. There is so little water in their composition that they will dry readily, without any tendency to decay, and the flavour is hardly to be equalled by any other.

Chantarelles are another kind which are admirably adapted for drying in the same manner as the foregoing, from which they also differ in the kind of flavour which they impart. If the specimens are large they should be cut in half before drying in order to facilitate the process.

The hedgehog mushroom (*Hydnum repandum*) is also available for the same purpose, but these should be cut or sliced, as whole specimens, if large, are liable to decay if dried too slowly. It would be preferable in all cases to slice them in the same manner as the *Boleti*.

The St George's mushroom (*Agaricus gambosus*) has been recommended for drying, but we have never tried it, since at the time of its appearance no other fungi are to be had, and it has never been our good fortune to have more at a time than we were glad to use for immediate consumption.

Some mycologists have commended the two related species, the plum mushroom (*Agaricus prunulus*) and the orcella (*Agaricus orcella*), as excellent for drying, but these seem to have such a delicate flavour, only appreciable if cooked whilst fresh, that we have almost regarded it as a sin " to waste their sweetness in the kitchen air " by the evaporation of their aroma in drying.

There are several other species of fleshy agarics which would dry very well, and answer the ordinary purpose of flavouring in winter, but they do not retain that delicacy which recommends them in the fresh state, and for such a purpose there are plenty of others. For instance, few would care to sacrifice such a breakfast delicacy as the parasol mushroom (*Agaricus procerus*) for the remote exigencies of a winter stew.

Foremost amongst the best kinds for the flavouring of winter dishes are the morels. We have several different species, but none of them too common, and the small ones may be dried on strings, entire, the larger cut into segments. It is a curious circumstance that the natives in the Vale of Cashmere and on the slopes of the Himalayas dry the morels on strings, in which form they are sold in the bazaars of North Western India as articles of food. One of the species is identical with one lately found in Scotland (*Morchella deliciosa*). They are dried in France and Italy, and we have purchased dried imported morels in Covent Garden market, but seldom seen fresh ones.

An excellent substitute, similar in flavour, are the *Helvellas*, which are more common with us, and at a later season of the year. The only two species large enough for drying (*Helvella crispa* and *Helvella lacunosa*) may be collected in such places as Epping Forest, during the autumn, and are perhaps more suitable for drying for winter use than for cooking when fresh. Often during an autumnal stroll one or two individuals will be found, and possibly no more, quite insufficient for a dish at the time, but they may be dried, and thus during a season quite a good supply may be obtained, one by one, or at most half a dozen at a time, and they will dry readily, anyhow, without any trouble, if left exposed to the air.

Truffles will, we fear, never be burdensome from their profusion, but in case any one should desire to experiment on drying them, they should be cut in slices about as thick as a penny, and if laid flat, be often turned over whilst drying, or the under surface is liable to moisten and decay. Dried truffles are not comparable with fresh ones, and even those preserved in oil are preferred by most persons, ourselves amongst the number. As a nation we are not great in truffle production, or in truffle eating, save in the guise of Strasburg pies.

Having dried such fungi as are intended to be preserved, thoroughly, they may be stored away in a dry place. Some have recommended wide mouthed bottles or jars, and others tin canisters or boxes, for holding the store, but our objection is to all hermetically sealed vessels, because the slightest amount of moisture present is sufficient to induce incipient mouldiness and a musty taste. We prefer muslin bags, or anything of the kind which permits of the ingress of air, and these suspended in the kitchen, or in a very dry place, will prove effectual. Only let dust be excluded, and the fungi kept thoroughly dry, but not air tight, as the latter may result in fermentation, or mouldiness, without any compensating advantage.

When any of the dried mushrooms are intended to be used they should be soaked for an hour in warm water, and then drained before using. Some prefer soaking all night. If added to a stew or soup, they should be the last ingredient, ten or fifteen minutes is sufficient. It is a great mistake to keep them boiling over the fire for an hour or two, and diffusing all the volatile flavour and aroma in steam.

We have already given instructions for the preparation of "mushroom powder" which needs not repetition. Our own experience of the best of this kind of preparation has not been satisfactory, but as others have spoken well of it, the fault may rest with ourselves.

In the metropolis dried "ceps" and dried mushrooms may be purchased at most of the shops for sale of German and Italian provisions, such as are found in the neighbourhood of Soho and Leicester Square.

XXXIV.—FUNGUS HUNTING.

FUNGUS eating of course implies fungus hunting, and as the articles to be consumed have first to be obtained, it is essential that all possible assistance should be given to attain this object. For this purpose it is essential that the inexperienced should know as well the times and seasons for certain species, and the most favourable localities, as to be able to discriminate them when found. Dealing as it does with a large number of different kinds of fungi, appearing consecutively through a period of some months, there must be some method in hunting

as well as in cooking, applicable to the different
kinds individually. It goes without saying that
some localities will be superior to others in their
facilities for obtaining the raw material, but the
worst localities will furnish a better result if worked
in a systematic manner, and as the edible fungi
under consideration are wild and spontaneous plants,
dependent not only upon terrestrial but also atmo-
spherical conditions, much time will be wasted, and
disappointment caused, if only a hap-hazard kind of
fungus hunting is resorted to. For instance, it will
be useless to make an excursion in the early summer
in the hope of finding kinds which do not make their
appearance until autumn, and it will be equally un-
availing to scour the woods in June for particular
species, such as the fairy ring champignon, which
does not grow in woods at all, but on open heaths,
lawns, parks, and pastures. In all such matters there
is no better guide than experience, but in default of
experience, and to assist in its acquisition, a little
may be communicated under the head of general
instructions.

Some excellent suggestions were made by Dr Bull
in a volume of the Woolhope Transactions as to the
period of the year in which the various edible fungi
prevail. He writes—"In the end of April, or the
beginning of May, the fungus season begins with the
appearance of the true St George's mushroom (*Agaricus
gambosus*) growing in fairy rings, in pastures. These

are quickly followed by the little fairy ring champignon (*Marasmius oreades*), scattered specimens of
the meadow mushroom, or horse mushroom (*Agaricus
arvensis*), clusters of the maned agaric (*Coprinus
comatus*), which in warm sunny seasons may be
gathered all through the months of May, June, and
July, and in the last month the edible boletus
(*Boletus edulis*) will have put in its appearance.
Then comes the great season of the common mushroom (*Agaricus campestris*), which may be allowed to
reign supreme through July and August. From this
time, through September and October, the great
crop of fungi will appear. Besides those already
named, there will abound the fine flavoured parasol
agaric (*Agaricus procerus*), the rich red milk agaric (*Lactarius deliciosus*), the brown warty agaric (*Agaricus
rubescens*), the great puff ball (*Lycoperdon giganteum*),
the vegetable beef steak (*Fistulina hepatica*) on decaying oak trees, vegetable sweet-bread (*Agaricus orcella*),
the plum mushroom (*Agaricus prunulus*), the pasture hygrophorus (*Hygrophorus pratensis*), and many
others. The seasons will then be carried on by the
hedgehog mushroom (*Hydnum repandum*), the small
but abundant ivory caps (*Hygrophorus virgineus*), the
blewits (*Agaricus personatus*), and the amethyst agaric
(*Agaricus nudus*), until the frosts of November and
December stop their growth." It might have been
added that even slight frosts do not materially affect
the different species of *Hygrophorus*, which are about

the last to linger, in defiance of the coming winter, except perhaps the pasture *Hygrophorus*, which is not a late species.

Under the different species we have given, together with the necessary descriptions for their identification, some intimation of their habitats. These will vary but little, although there will be some variation in the period of their advent, consequent upon the peculiarities of the season. Sometimes we have, as of late, a succession of seasons so unfavourable to the growth of fleshy fungi that they are comparatively rare throughout the year. At other times continuous warm, moist weather ensures a plentiful supply of one species after another for many months.

Hunting in woods for edible fungi should be undertaken later in the year than in the "open," and then it will save time if a few generalities are kept in remembrance. Where the ground is covered with bracken, or overrun with brambles, or has a dense growth of underwood, labour will be in vain. A very few of the smaller agarics may occasionally be found sparingly amongst bracken and bramble, but as a rule the experienced hunter passes such spots, on the assumption that they are absolutely barren. Dense undergrowth is not quite so bad, but only a few specimens are to be seen. The sides of paths, or rides, on the contrary, will usually furnish something of use or interest. Aspect is another point for consideration ; a southern or western aspect is far prefer-

able to an eastern or northern one. The cold northern side of a wood only affords a few of the hardiest
species, but a warm moist slope, facing the south or
the west, is usually a happy hunting ground. If the
season is a very dry one the bottom of the slopes,
and all damp spots should be explored. Cleared
spots, where the undergrowth has been cut down,
presents such a changed condition that it is useless to
walk over it for two or three years after the clearing
has taken place.

The majority of our woods are mixed woods, but
plantations of fir trees are useful in their way,
although the fungi are confined to a few species.
The fungi of fir woods will soon be recognised as
different from those in mixed woods, whilst such
things as yellow boleti and the red milk agaric
(*Lactarius deliciosus*) will only be found under fir trees.

The tree-loving species are also a little eccentric in
their habits. The slimy white species found so
constantly on beech trunks (*Agaricus mucidus*) will
be seen scattered in clusters all over a dead beech
trunk whilst still standing, but only sparingly when
the trunk is prostrate. In some woods prostrate
timber is not allowed to be on the ground long
enough to produce a good crop of fungi, but, when
permitted, the oyster mushroom (*Agaricus ostreatus*)
will be found in large, dense clusters. We have
never been successful in finding it elsewhere than on
fallen timber, whereas the elm tree mushroom

(*Agaricus ulmarius*) flourishes high up on the rotting branches of standing elms, and we do not remember having collected it from a prostrate elm.

When parks and pastures are explored no one would dream of undertaking it at times when continuous drought has turned the grass yellow, and hardened the ground so that fungi cannot penetrate above the surface. At all times care should be taken to look under the shadow of all the trees, and especially around the circle of drip from the outer branches. As a rule the number of species of all kinds found in open places is much less than of those occurring in woods, but this is compensated by the species being of a different kind. Low lying, damp meadows are unproductive, the preference being given to old parks and commons. It need scarcely to be suggested that quiet and secluded places are to be preferred, and not such as are infested by the British public for picnics, where the ground is trodden down, all toadstools kicked over and destroyed, with a legacy of luncheon papers, meat tins, and empty bottles to mark the track of the spoilers.

In gathering fungi for domestic purposes some prefer an open basket, whilst others, with a strong regard for appearances, select in preference a tin vasculum, such as is used for collecting plants for botanical purposes. In either case it is quite unnecessary to carry more than is requisite. The stems can always be cut off close to the gills, and discarded, and then the caps may be packed close together in a comparatively small space, preference always being given to young, fresh looking individuals, rigidly excluding all which exhibit a tendency to decay, or are attacked by insects. It is of no consequence the mixing of several kinds together for the purpose of transit, but these should be separated afterwards, as we have no sympathy with the practice of combining two or three kinds together to furnish a dish for the table. Each kind should be tested on its own merits, and not combined into a sort of mushroom Irish stew. Again, we repeat that " the fresher the better " applies to all esculent fungi, and that the sooner they are cooked the better.

Neither can we omit to caution the reckless against being reckless with articles of food. We have given as clear a definition as we could of each species, and have added figures of a large number, so that any one, with the exercise of moderate care and intelligence, may with certainty determine, without risk, the species we have named. If at any time there should be a doubt, let the benefit be given to the doubt, and either relinquish the dish or call in the assistance of some one more experienced to set the doubt at rest. We do not approve of experiments in fungus eating, and hence we have included none which we were not perfectly sure were entirely safe. It is an excellent plan to select a few species at first, and learn to know them well, before proceeding to others, unless the others are recommended and determined by some one of experience. There is no better method than to join in some fungus foray, which is usually conducted by some capable person, and endeavour to have the edible species pointed out, so that they may be examined and compared with descriptions and figures. In this way all hesitation is removed, and those particular species become as well known as the face of an old and familiar friend.

XXXV.—LIST OF EDIBLE FUNGI.

DRY and uninteresting as an inventory, or catalogue, will be a barren list of the fungi of Britain available for domestic purposes, and yet we are about to venture upon it as a direct means of proving that the subject has not been exhausted. Of course we do not expect any one to read it, but some infatuated individual may at some remote period be induced to consult it, perhaps with the charitable hope of finding it wrong, or making suggestions for its improvement. It must not be concluded that all are equally delicate, or appetizing ; it is sufficient for this purpose that the species is recognized as edible. Their respective merits must be determined by individual tastes. Some are prefixed by an asterisk (*) to indicate that we have eaten them ourselves and still survive to testify to the fact. The adoption of scientific names was a necessity in order to secure accuracy and promote recognition by those who prefer precision in matters of life and death.

*Agaricus (Amanita) rubescens. *Fries.*

Agaricus (Amanita) strobiliformis. *Vitt.*

*Agaricus (Amanitopsis) vaginatus. *Bull.*

*Agaricus (Lepiota) procerus. *Scop.*

*Agaricus (Lepiota) rachodes. *Vitt.*

Agaricus (Lepiota) excoriatus. *Schæff.*

Agaricus (Lepiota) gracilentus. *Kromb.*

Agaricus (Lepiota) mastoideus. *Fries.* Small, and not very strongly recommended.

*Agaricus (Lepiota) acutesquamosus. *Weinm.*

Agaricus (Lepiota) naucinus. *Fries.*

Agaricus (Lepiota) holosericeus. *Fries.*

*Agaricus (Armillaria) melleus. *Fl. Dan.* Very common, and much used on the Continent, but not recommended.

*Agaricus (Armillaria) mucidus. *Schrad.*

Agaricus (Tricholoma) flavo-brunneus. *Fries.*

Agaricus (Tricholoma) russula. *Schæff.*

Agaricus (Tricholoma) columbetta. *Fries.*

Agaricus (Tricholoma) imbricatus. *Fries.*

*Agaricus (Tricholoma) gambosus. *Fries.*

Agaricus (Tricholoma) amethystinus. *Scop.*

Agaricus (Tricholoma) albellus. *Fries.*

Agaricus (Tricholoma) tigrinus. *Schæff.*

Agaricus (Tricholoma) pes caprœ. *Fries.*

Agaricus (Tricholoma) arcuatus. *Bull.*

*Agaricus (Tricholoma) personatus. *Fries.*

*Agaricus (Tricholoma) nudus. *Bull.*

Agaricus (Tricholoma) grammopodius. *Bull.*

Agaricus (Tricholoma) brevipes. *Bull.*

Agaricus (Tricholoma) acerbus. *Fries.* Is said to be eaten on the Continent, but we know of no one who has tried it.

*Agaricus (Clitocybe) nebularis. *Batsch.*

*Agaricus (Clitocybe) opiparus. *Fries.*

Agaricus (Clitocybe) oderus. *Bull.*

Agaricus (Clitocybe) cerussatus. *Fries.*

*Agaricus (Clitocybe) dealbatus. *Sow.*

Agaricus (Clitocybe) fumosus. *Pers.*

Agaricus (Clitocybe) monstrosus. *Sow.*

Agaricus (Clitocybe) maximus. *Fries.*

Agaricus (Clitocybe) giganteus. *Sow.*

*Agaricus (Clitocybe) infundibuliformis. *Fries.*

*Agaricus (Clitocybe) geotropus. *Bull.*

Agaricus (Clitocybe) subinvolutus. *Batsch.*

Agaricus (Clitocybe) gilvus. *Pers.*

*Agaricus (Clitocybe) catinus. *Fries.*

Agaricus (Clitocybe) cyathiformis. *Fries.*

Agaricus (Clitocybe) expallens. *Pers.*

Agaricus (Clitocybe) obbatus. *Fries.*

Agaricus (Clitocybe) pruinosus. *Lasch.*

Agaricus (Clitocybe) brumalis. *Fries.*

*Agaricus (Clitocybe) fragrans. *Sow.*

Agaricus (Clitocybe) laccatus. *Scop.*

*Agaricus (Collybia) fusipes. *Bull.*

Agaricus (Collybia) esculentus. *Wulf.*

Agaricus (Pleurotus) dryinus. *Pers.*

*Agaricus (Pleurotus) ulmarius. *Bull.*

*Agaricus (Pleurotus) sapidus. *Kalch.*

*Agaricus (Pleurotus) ostreatus. *Jacq.*

*Agaricus (Pleurotus) euosmus. *Berk.*

Agaricus (Pleurotus) glandulosus. *Bull.*

Agaricus (Pleurotus) salignus. *Pers.* Should only be eaten when young.

Agaricus (Pleurotus) petaloides. *Bull.*

Agaricus (Pleurotus) pulmonarius. *Fries.* Has been recommended, but is very rare.

Agaricus (Volvaria) bombycinus. *Schæff.* Is often eaten abroad, but we have never been induced to try it. Pink spored species are (as a rule) suspicious.

Agaricus (Entoloma) rhodopolius. *Fries.*

*Agaricus (Clitopilus) prunulus. *Scop.*

*Agaricus (Clitopilus) orcella. *Bull.*

Agaricus (Clitopilus) popinalis. *Fries.*

Agaricus (Pholiota) præcox. *Pers.*

Agaricus (Pholiota) pudicus. *Fries.*

*Agaricus (Pholiota) leochromus. *Cooke.*

Agaricus (Pholiota) ægerita. *Fries.*

Agaricus (Pholiota) squarrosus. *Mull.* Cordier

recommends this, but we should doubt if it is worth the trouble of cooking.

Agaricus (Pholiota) mutabilis. *Schœff.* Certainly edible, but not delicate.

A garicus (Psalliota) elvensis. *Berk.*

*Agaricus (Psalliota) arvensis. *Schœff.*

Agaricus (Psalliota) pratensis. *Schœff.*

Agaricus (Psalliota) cretaceus. *Fries.*

Agaricus (Psalliota) campestris. *Linn.*

*Agaricus (Psalliota) sylvaticus. *Schœff.*

Agaricus (Psalliota) hæmorrhoidarius. *Kalch.*

Agaricus (Hypholoma) velutinus. *Pers.*

Agaricus (Hypholoma) candolleanus. *Fries.* The latter two species are often introduced as an ingredient in catsup, but, although innocent and edible, we doubt if many persons would consider them good enough.

*Coprinus comatus. *Fries.*

*Coprinus atramentarius. *Fries.*

Coprinus sterquilinus. *Fries.*

Cortinarius (Phlegmacium) varius. *Fries.*

Cortinarius (Phlegmacium) turbinatus. *Bull.*

Cortinarius (Myxacium) collinitus. *Fries.*

Cortinarius (Inoloma) violaceus. *Fries.*

Cortinarius (Telamonia) armillatus. *Fries.*

Cortinarius (Telamonia) hœmatochelis. *Bull.*

Cortinarius (Dermocybe) cinnamomeus. *Fries.*

Cortinarius (Hydrocybe) castaneus. *Bull.*

*Gomphidius glutinosus. *Schœff.*

*Gomphidius viscidus. *Linn.*

These two species of Gomphidius are chiefly used in the manufacture of catsup.

*Paxillus involutus. *Batsch.*

*Hygrophorus eburneus. *Bull.*

Hygrophorus penarius. *Fries.*

Hygrophorus erubescens. *Fries.*

*Hygrophorus pratensis. *Pers.*

*Hygrophorus virgineus. *Wulf.*

*Hygrophorus niveus. *Scop.*

*Hygrophorus coccineus. *Schœff.*

Hygrophorus puniceus. *Fries.*

*Lactarius turpis. *Fries.*

Lactarius controversus. *Fries.*

These two species are rather deficient in aroma and flavour.

Lactarius utilis. *Weinm.*

Lactarius pergamenus. *Fries.*

Lactarius piperatus. *Scop.*

These two species of Lactarius are eaten on the Continent and in the United States, but have hitherto been regarded as suspicious in this country.

*Lactarius deliciosus. *Linn.*

Lactarius pallidus. *Pers.*

Lactarius quietus. *Fries.*

Lactarius volemus. *Fries.*

*Lactarius mitissimus. *Fries.*

*Lactarius subdulcis. *Bull.*

Lactarius camphoratus. *Bull.*

Russula lactea. *Fries.*

*Russula virescens. *Schœff.*

Russula lepida. *Fries.*

Russula vesca. *Fries.*

*Russula cyanoxantha. *Schœff.*

*Russula heterophylla. *Fries.*

Russula integra. *Linn.*

Russula alutacea. *Fries.*

*Cantharellus cibarius. *Fries.*

*Marasmius oreades. *Fries.*

Marasmius scorodonius. *Fries.*

Lentinus tigrinus. *Fries.*

Panus conchatus. *Fries.*

Panus torulosus. *Fries.*

These latter three species are tough when old, and never very delicate or digestible.

Boletus luteus. *Linn.*

Boletus elegans. *Schum.*

*Boletus granulatus. *Linn.*

Boletus bovinus. *Linn.*

Boletus badius. *Fries.*

*Boletus edulis. *Bull.*

Boletus aereus. *Bull.*

Boletus vaccinus. *Fries.*

Boletus fragrans. *Vitt.*

Boletus impolitus. *Fries.*

Boletus aestivalis. *Fries.*

*Boletus versipellis. *Fries.*

*Boletus scaber. *Fries.*

*Boletus castaneus. *Fries.*

Polyporus frondosus. *Fries.*

*Polyporus intybaceus. *Fries.*

These Polypori should only be attempted when young and juicy, and then only the pilei.

*Fistulina hepatica. *Fries.*

Hydnum imbricatum. *Linn.*

*Hydnum repandum. *Linn.*

Hydnum coralloides. *Scop.*

Hydnum erinaceum. *Bull.*

Hydnum caput medusæ. *Bull.*

Tremellodon gelatinosum. *Fries.*

*Craterellus cornucopioides. *Pers.*

*Sparassis crispa. *Fries.*

Clavaria flava. *Schæff.*

Clavaria botrytes. *Pers.*

Clavaria amethystina. *Bull.*

Clavaria fastigiata. *Linn.*

Clavaria coralloides. *Linn.*

*Clavaria cristata. *Fries.*

Clavaria cinerea. *Bull.*

*Clavaria rugosa. *Bull.*

Clavaria aurea. *Schæff.*

*Clavaria vermicularis. *Scop.*

Clavaria pistillaris. *Linn.*

Hirneola auricula-Judææ. *Fries.* Is used by the Chinese as an ingredient in soups.

Tremella lutescens. *Pers.*

Tremella mesenterica. *Retz.*

These two species of *Tremella* are usually too small to be of any value as an esculent.

Bovista plumbea. *Fries.* (Young).

*Lycoperdon giganteum. *Batsch.*

Lycoperdon gemmatum. *Fries.*

Lycoperdon perlatum. *Pers.*

All these puff balls must be eaten only when young, white, and juicy.

*Morchella esculenta. *Pers.*

*Morchella conica. *Pers.*

*Morchella Smithiana. *Cooke.*

Morchella deliciosa. *Fries.*

Morchella gigas. *Pers.*

Morchella crassipes. *Pers.*

Morchella semilibera. *D. Cand.*

*Helvella crispa. *Fries.*

*Helvella lacunosa. *Afz.*

Helvella elastica. *Bull.*

Peziza acetabulum. *Linn.*

Peziza macropus. *Pers.*

*Peziza vesiculosa. *Bull.*

Peziza aurantia. *Vahl.*

*Peziza venosa. *Pers.*

Peziza cochleata. *Bull.*

Peziza badia. *Pers.*

Peziza cerea. *Sow.*

*Tuber æstivum. *Vitt.*

Tuber mesentericum. *Tul.*

Tuber brumale. *Mich.*

Melanogaster variegatus. *Tul.*

INDEX.

TURNBULL AND SPEARS, PRINTERS, EDINBURGH.